envision

experiencing the world from the inside out

envision

experiencing the world from the inside out

by
Peter E. Matthews

preface by Bishop Vinton R. Anderson

edited by Alexis M. Dobbins

writeRelations.com | P.O. Box 7683 | Largo, MD 20792

Copyright © 2006 by writeRelations.com, Publishers, P.O. Box 7683, Largo, MD 20792. All rights reserved. No part of this publication may be reproduced, stored in a retrieval system, or transmitted, in any form or by any means, electronic, mechanical, photocopying, recording, or otherwise, without the prior written permission of the publisher. All rights reserved.

To contact writeRelations.com directly, call 240.691.4473 or visit our website at www.writeRelations.com.

Discounts on bulk quantities of writeRelations.com books are available to corporations, professional, and civic associations. For details and discount information, contact the Sales Department at writeRelations.com .

This book contains information gathered from many sources. Neither the author nor the publishers engaged in rendering any legal, psychological, or accounting advice. The authors and publisher disclaim any personal liability, either directly or indirectly, for advice or information presented. They assume no responsibility for errors, inaccuracies, omissions, or any inconsistency herein. Any slights of people, places, publishers, books, or organizations are unintentional.

Library of Congress Catologing-in-Publication data is available.

ISBN 978-0-9771083-1-2

Cover Photo - T. Jerrod Sharpe
Cover Design - Dennis Laffoon

10 9 8 7 6 5 4 3 2 1

Peter E. Matthews
Author

*Confessions: Inside the Complex Soul
of a Thug Pastor (2003)*

*Passin' the Plate: Offerings of Hope and Healing for
Humanity (2005)*

To **Bishop Vinton R. Anderson**
whose vision in creating his fellowship
has unleashed my ecumenical imagination
and opened potential doors
too many to number.

To **my fiancée Pam**
whose unyielding love and commitment
continues to inspire me
to envision
a better life
in the best possible world

TABLE OF CONTENTS

Preface 1
An Intimate Journey Towards Authenticity 3
   Prayer of Authenticity 9
Becoming Who the World Needs and God Desires 10
Ecumenical Reflections of the Heart 14
   Blazin' from the Inside Out 16
   MJB Global Chorus 20
   Gift of Hope is No Laughing Matter 23
   Calling for an Internal Referendum 28
   Somewhere Between Here and There 33
Ecumenical Reflections of the Mind 38
   Prayer of Mental Reflection 40
   A New Day is Dawning 42
   A Way of Life 60
Ecumenical Reflections of the Soul 78
   Prayer of Soulful Reflection 80
   Standing on the Shoulders of Giants 82
Envision – Seven Steps to Authenticity 108
   Prayer of Envisioning 111
   Equip 112
   Negotiate 115
   Vision 118
   Integrity 121
   Submit 125
   Innovate 128
   Optimize 131
   Navigate 134

𝒮

PREFACE

Ministry to the whole people of God in a didactic mode is an enormously difficult task. The difficulty is apparent because it seems more natural to focus on our particularities than on an ecumenical agenda.

How do we develop an epistemology that relates to the whole inhabited earth, when we are so preoccupied with the specifics of our own dilemmas, and the drives we promote for the benefit of a few?

Nevertheless, Peter Matthews has determined both by word and deed to accomplish this endeavor beginning with *Envision: Experiencing the World from the Inside Out*. Not only is he living in an ecumenical house, known as the Bossey Ecumenical Institute in Geneva, Switzerland, where he is a candidate for an advanced degree in Ecumenics, but he has accepted the challenge to research and delineate a methodology by which the human family can be drawn closer together.

Convinced that he is called to an ecumenical destiny, Peter has opened himself to serve the wider community by bringing new hope as set forth in John 17.

It pleases me that the Vinton R. Anderson Ecumenical Leadership Scholarship has allowed Rev. Matthews to broaden his vision and hopefully others will follow.

Bishop Vinton R. Anderson
Former President, World Council of Churches

1

Psalm 51, v1-11

Have mercy on me, O God, according to your unfailing love;

according to your great compassion blot out my transgressions.

Wash away all my iniquity

and cleanse me from my sin.

For I know my transgressions,

and my sin is always before me.

Against you, you only, have I sinned and done what is evil in your sight, so that you are proved right when you speak and justified when you judge.

Surely I was sinful at birth, sinful from the time my mother conceived me.

Surely you desire truth in the inner parts

you teach me wisdom in the inmost place.

Cleanse me with hyssop, and I will be clean;

wash me, and I will be whiter than snow.

Let me hear joy and gladness;

let the bones you have crushed rejoice.

Hide your face from my sins and blot out all my iniquity.

Create in me a pure heart, O God,

and renew a steadfast spirit within me.

Do not cast me from your presence or take your Holy Spirit from me.

Restore to me the joy of your salvation and grant me a willing spirit,

to sustain me.

✍

INTRODUCTION

<u>An Intimate Journey Towards Authenticity</u>

This is my third publication in as many years. Writing for me has become as important as breathing because it provides for me the emotional oxygen needed to make sense of my role as a steward in God's creation. Much like a poor man's therapy, writing has provided an outlet for dialogue where I am challenged in constructive and meaningful ways as well. As I look back over the last three years of my life I am humbled not only because of the support I have received, but also because of the path of maturation that I have traveled while striving to find practical ways to live out the meaning of my favorite word in the English language. Authentic.

> The number of ministers who are perfectly realistic about their tasks and who are sincerely anxious to help the modern generation find itself, not only in the intricate problems of the personal life but in the moral and social complexities of society, is much larger man than the critics of the church are able to know are willing to concede.[1]

My first book *Confessions: Inside the Complex Soul of a Thug Pastor* afforded the opportunity to present myself to a wider secular audience as a human being. In my last year as pastor of an inner-city church in Ohio I wrote a newspaper column for the largest African American newspaper in the Buckeye state. The newspaper column was written under the pseudonym "Thug Pastor". As the column's topics were unlimited the response both to the paper and my private email account was overwhelming.

Sex.

Depression.

Global Poverty.

Foreign Policy. Sex.

Politics. Leadership. Sex.

Hip-Hop Culture.

Did I mention Sex? Yet, when I revealed my identity and folded the columns into my first book, *Confessions*, the reaction from the church community in particular was astonishingly mixed.

Church folks were astonished by my "vulgar" language, but privately lauded me for *keeping it real.*

They were "put off" by vivid disclosures about the past and current status of my sex life. Yet, countless numbers of them with children and grandchildren in tow (90% not members of my parish) privately visited my office often without appointment to discuss the *birds and the bees* in a language that bridged the gap across generations.

Speaking engagements and media appearances rolled in, but this popularity did not result in the type of congregational growth my former church desired. Now crack addicts and drug dealers were regular visitors. Homeless people, alcoholics, and those recently freed from prison sought out our church's extensive community outreach programs as a refuge from the harsh winds of a neighborhood turned into ghost town as a result of the increasing violence and constant crime. This was far from the type of exposure and publicity the elders of the church expected from their Ivy League trained pastor.

As a result of personal immaturity and an unwillingness to change, migraines and hemorrhoids had become occupational hazards. My physical weight rapidly spun out of control as fast as my personal life. Looking for ways to maintain a developing reputation without a hobby to call my own, my personal and professional decision making ability was completely impaired. I felt rejected in an environment where elder members had conveniently forgotten the poverty of their recent past and the newer members from the community were not yet in a position to contribute to the life line of the congregation. My overwhelming need for external validation was doing more than costing me members, and I was slowly losing my mind.

I shall never forget September 11, 2004, the morning of my 32nd birthday. I looked in the mirror and wept. I had become what I despised.

Disgruntled and disillusioned I applied for M.A. & Ph.D. programs in Switzerland on a humble. The World Council of Churches and The University of Geneva had recently cemented a unique partnership at the WCC Bossey Ecumenical Institute in Celigny, Switzerland.

The Bossey Institute had become an *Ecumenical Laboratory* for over fifty years for people from all over the world. By ecumenical, we mean that Bossey had taken individuals from untold numbers of Christian denominations the world over and created a Graduate School where pastors, professors, and lay people alike could critically engage one another and common texts for the purposes of advancing Christian unity. American Baptists and Coptics from Russia. German Lutherans and Anglicans from Kenya were educated in the ways of religious diplomacy in an effort to breach centuries of culture differences and historic misgivings.

At the close of the church fiscal year, I began the application process. Humbly waiting five months for a potential acceptance letter, and then another five months to lock down the $25,000.00 needed for tuition, fees, room, board, and living expenses. I was officially unemployed and unable to clearly assess my current reality or my ultimate purpose.

No longer a pastor, all of the fringe benefits associated with my previous vocation came to a screeching halt. No more radio or television interviews. Speaking engagements became close to non-existent as the possibility of pulpit reciprocity no longer presented itself, but I kept writing. Writing provided me with the opportunity to explore the depth of my personal uncertainty. Having suffered from burnout at the age of 32, I still had a son to provide for and bills to pay.

My next move was to offer "my services" as a church consultant for three congregations in the greater Washington, D.C. area as I prayed to God and awaited word on my acceptance. Yet, I kept writing.

As a consultant I was again afforded the luxury of teaching, preaching, and attempting to create systems that would enrich the qualities of people's lives but this time without the responsibility of the pastoral follow through. I was able to playa' hate and get away with it.

My second publication, *Passin' The Plate: Offerings of Hope and Healing for Humanity* speaks to my enlightened jealousy. My feelings were akin to that of a luxurious car detail shop owner, but one without the opportunity to provide regular maintenance (oil change, brake replacement, or rotary belts) for any of the cars on the lot. In my consultation I was able to witness the seasoned saints and prominent pastors who continued to envelope themselves in "ministries" while not confronting the depth of their pain or the width of their demons. *Passin' the Plate* provided an opportunity to talk with (primarily) persons of colors about the frustration felt in churches; however, my own pain had not yet allowed me to facilitate conversations that would enable healing. Sophisticated playa hating had become a lucrative venture, and then God hooked me up with a $20,000.00 fellowship for school.

Barbershops. Beauty Salons. Black Student Unions. Independent book stores. Private Homes. And of course, churches. All these public spaces were excited to have yet another preacher beat up on the church, because people of all colors, sexes, educational backgrounds, and income levels are in serious pain. A pain that spirals into numbness as persons feel their respective houses of worship are not speaking consistently to their ever growing confusion and bewilderment.

Much more than being purpose driven, people are longing to contribute as well. Many of us know people who attend Mega Fest, own every Yolanda Adams' CD, daily watch popular televangelists, and still hurt. This second publication poured gasoline on open wounds, and provided a jolt in the fractured ego of a tormented writer looking for a soft landing.

Passin' the Plate provoked intense discussion. Starburst colors-suited preachers and D.O.G. training techniques for women sparked charged conversations, but did not necessarily spawn any action or testimonies. I had fallen in the trap that so many of our young ambitious men do. I had found a way to sensationalize and market the obvious.

Yet, while in revival in Dothan, Alabama numb arms and chest pains left me drenched with sweat and severe headaches. What I assumed was a stroke turned out to be acid reflux and high blood pressure.

The time away from pastorship had provided exposure, but not introspection. Three weeks away from leaving the country and I was faced with another hard truth on my birthday. Tears flowed once again as the realization came that you can neither hide nor run from yourself. Pardon any unintended vanity or pomposity, but in a very Christ-like fashion my 33rd birthday became the year of a slow painful death. In my rebirth I finally began to imagine, to conceive, to picture as possible. I finally began to *envision*.

Less than six weeks into my tenure overseas my life finally caught up with me. The lies and the affairs. The financial difficulties and the health issues. No longer able to hide behind a woman, a sermon, or a book signing, the time to confront my destiny had arrived. *"As the deer pants for streams of water, so my soul pants for you, O God. My soul thirsts for the living God. When can I go and meet with God? My tears have been my food day and night"* (Psalm 42:1-2). Bridges had been burned and relationships had been destroyed, but I kept writing.

In my thirst for God I now began to diligently seek the contents of the plate I proclaimed to be passing all over the country. School provided the context to discover that the pain was not mine alone. Indeed, people spanning the world were enduring similar trials. My tears proved to be the nutrient needed to endure the pain of self-discovery, and the sober environment unleashed a tsunami of love that can only be articulated as grace. I began to envision, because I was finally ready to both *receive* and *be* a blessing all at the same time. What about you? Are you ready to quit hatin' and be a blessing? Let's get to work!

ENVISION

Dear God,

Something is missing from our lives and in this world! For as we look out into Your world we see chaos all around, and we need a new reality that will instruct us to combat the evil forces from without as well as those that lie within.

Give us a new reality that teaches us to deal with global warming in Darfur as well as Denmark. Poverty rates continue to deny Your children the realization of their innate genius. Teach us how to equip the next generation of leaders in Iraq as well as Indianapolis. Disease robs Your mothers of adequate means to fend for themselves in hostile environments of violence and neglect. Lord, unleash new possibilities for single mothers in Hattiesburg as well as Haiti. Lord, we need you!

Yet, we must also be instructed in the ways of holiness. We must again learn that our bodies are our temples as we exert pressure to end the AIDS pandemic. We must learn that our mouths in idle chatter shed as much innocent blood as any suicide bomber. Help us to learn how we must unlock the latent compassion stored in our souls to be as righteous as we are revolutionary. In this way we foster the change by the life we live. In this way we model behaviors that we seek to inspire.

In this way we begin to ENVISION more than just a new world order, but a new way of living as well. A new reality where we can stop running away from oppression and our past. The formation of a place where we can embrace our shortcomings as glimpses of the ways in which broken people will soon find wholeness.

Help us, Lord to ENVISION a new world by finding the daily courage of our convictions to change our own.

In your Son's name we pray
Amen
Amen
Amen

᪅

CHAPTER 1

Becoming Who The World Needs and God Desires

"Many men (and women) lead lives of quiet desperation and die with a song still in them," says Henry David Thoreau. Many of us who will read this are educated, employed, retired, or otherwise equipped to be the conduits of planet altering realities. Yet, we are unable to locate the continual energy to release our respective passions. Members of somebody's church, we have yet to become consumed with a sense of joy that will unlock the inner demons most often called guilt and apathy.

To locate that passion you must be as curious as you are compassionate. You must be disciplined and determined. Within the recesses of your soul lie cures to diseases, patents for inventions, and a business plan that would change the course of your family's history for generations! Why did I begin this ecumenical journey with such intense and personal reflections? To serve as a simple reminder that you are not alone! In Jesus very public and humiliating death he put his enemies on notice as to the extent of the power that was soon to be entrusted to Him by the Father! I am finally singing! Are you?!

One must know from the outset that the process of envisioning does not include a religious laundry lists of do's and don'ts. It is a way of life that focuses your heart, mind, and soul on the daily practice of ensuring that the world is a better place as a result of you passing through. It means reading more than your local newspaper as part of a devotional that grows into a witness whereby those around you will learn about the complex world we live in. It requires that your health becomes an essential priority because not knowing is no longer an excuse. Indeed, you must avail yourselves to live a sober lifestyle with enough courage to endure the pangs of transformative process without the addictive characteristics, personality flaws, or behavior that up until now shaped your character. You must be finally ready to cry for the right reasons.

"The eyes of the Lord are on the righteous and his ears are attentive to their cry" (Psalm 34:15). What do I mean by sober? What are your addictions? Unrealized potential? Excessive spending? Useless activities? The pangs of withdrawing from a life-style of external validation mean more than learning to love yourself and reading a five minute devotional over your morning coffee with Matt Lauer and The Today Show. Yes, it means more than loving you. It means learning to be <u>with</u> you as well. With yourself, you will encounter the fear of being found out, resentment, painful admissions, and require a great deal of patience from those who profess to be closest to you.

Patience while you get that degree you should have gotten 10 years ago, but blamed your children instead. Patience as you dedicate yourself to read and suggest the book club read something other than another fiction book with the same plot by a different author. Your pain was merely preparation for your destiny, and now you are prepared to unleash what was placed in you before you were born. *"Before I formed you in the womb I knew you, before you were born I set you apart...." (Jeremiah 1:5)* What does the voice of sobriety sound like? How does a life-style dedicated to the way of envisioning look? How can you experience the world from the inside out without ever boarding a plane?

The balance of this initial chapter represents my first public series of sober reflections. Am I perfect? Hell no! See what I mean? These ecumenical reflections represent my remarkably good fortune to experience an increasingly small world from within. Switzerland. Germany. Italy. The Vatican (and yes, there is a difference). Spain. France. Twenty-five additional countries experienced through the souls of some the most amazing people the Church has to offer. As you mutually read and experience this book my earnest prayer is that you permit your increasingly sober Spirit to soar to places of which you never dreamed or imagined.

Spending the last ten months with some thirty people from more than twenty-five countries has led my heart, mind, and soul to dream big dreams again while focusing on one central fact.

Suffering does not discriminate. Suffering causes individuals to cry warmed-over tears and hostile nations to engage in warmed-over battles for supremacy. It shows no partiality to denomination, creed, or doctrine. The color of Pentecostal Clifford from Nigeria's tears are the same as those of Methodist Lousiale from Tonga. Amongst these thirty people I discovered that in each of our individual quests to envision a new reality we were all made aware that we were Wounded Healers.

In an attempt to guide you through your quest, to facilitate your changing the world through the mirror of your soul, let us look at our ecumenical reflections. Of the heart, mind, and soul, these reflections are to be taken as meditations for those unafraid and unashamed to think critically. There will be no naming or claiming in the forthcoming pages; instead, there reflections are intended to incite thought and discussion through further study and journaling. Developed to inspire action and solidarity, many believe the international ecumenical movement died with the introduction of the modern American civil rights movement. Others see the pursuit of organic church unity as neither relevant nor possible at a time when the Church, seemingly, fails to influence an ever-growing global economic machine with no ethics and few morals. Come with me now, as I attempt to offer solid examples and a concrete road map for your heart, head, and soul. Let us change the world in the midst of changing ourselves. God is watching! The world is waiting! Come... let us begin to envision together.

❧

CHAPTER 2

Ecumenical Reflections of the Heart

Where Paris, Mary J. Blige, and Malcolm X hook up

Here you are in my heart's chambers through a series of blogs I posted on the internet during my Graduate program at the Bossey Ecumenical Institute. Presented in an international context, it serves as my humble attempt to merge the critical issues of the day into an opportunity for reflection.

At a time when the Pentecostal movement in Christendom is on the eve a of a potential World War III in the Middle East...I could not think of a more apt way in which people of faith should think of themselves. The Sustainer of the Universe requires more from us than shouting, clapping, and dancing. In this series of essays, popular culture and historical figures are used to glean information as well as inspiration. We have been set apart to offer a more human face to the course of human history!

Our hearts will offer to the world a genuine compassion that seeks to work through the tears that pioneers will inevitably have to endure. In this chapter we seek to provide your heart with the information needed to act. What actions are being prompted by your heart these days?

15

ENVISION

Dear God,

Lord, open our hearts and help them to think!

As we step out into a world enveloped with information allow our hearts to put the pieces together. Give our hearts the ability to recognize the difference between the authentic and the hypocrite. Allow our hearts that have anxiously waited for love beyond our emotions find a passion to live for. Unleash gentleness in our hearts' secret chamber that causes us to both say quiet prayers when ambulances pass and cry secret tears when we see innocent children in Pakistan forced to attend school in unheard-of temperatures.

Lord, help us to love again!

That we might show just as much patience with leaders who have slipped from pedestals the same way as you show patience toward us as we struggle with our private addictions. Guide us as we stand in prayer with people from different faith backgrounds, and learn that the true intent of Your love is grounded in sincere respect not judgment. Baptize our hearts that we may repent of ambition and isolation just as we do from adultery and idolatry. For when our hearts begin to think we will create structures of equality and equity. As our hearts begin to breathe we will work tirelessly to assist in the regions devastated by earthquakes, floods, and tsunamis.

Lord, open our hearts and help them to think! For only then will our efforts to serve be met with Your righteous approval! For we are not our brother's keeper! We are not our sister's keeper. We are all One in You. Thus, as You create space in our heart to help them…

You are creating space in someone else's heart to help us.

In Your Son's name we pray,

Amen

Amen

Amen

16

Blazin' from the Inside Out

November 5, 2005

Yesterday at breakfast the ghost of the late prophetic Black polemic James Baldwin quickened my spirit as I read Friday morning's *International Herald Tribune.* He said; "**If we do not now dare everything, the fulfillment of that prophecy, re-created from the Bible in song by a slave, is upon us:** *God gave Noah the rainbow sign, No more water, the fire next time!!*"

Paris, France is on fire! The birthplace of Alexis De Tocqueville, Thomas Hobbes, and countless petty-bourgeoisie armchair intellectuals is blazing'! As of this moment over 14 suburbs of Paris, France are currently enveloped in flames. Early reports have over 1200 cars torched, at least three nurseries bombed, and statements last night indicate that an elderly woman was set afire after being dragged from a bus stop. Some 2300 policemen and countless French firemen have been deployed to both confront and extinguish a powder keg whose fuse was lit long ago.

Masses of young men of color from Paris, France, to Porto Allegro, Brazil and Pittsburgh, USA have long sought creative entry into a world that views them as some sort of labor. It is no coincidence (nor should it be any surprise) that when two teenagers of African ancestry were electrocuted while hiding from French police in a power substation……trouble was imminent. The despair of the northern African adolescent male population in Paris is seen in the yearning for educational opportunities, job training initiatives, and courageous leadership that stop speaking to their fears *(insert votes)* as opposed to their faith *(insert vision)*.

Have you indeed *dared everything* in your evolving attempts to equip, enrich, and empower young people across this world? Precisely, why Baldwin's quote must be analyzed in the context in which it was produced. The book was published in 1963 after both Dr. Martin Luther King Jr. shared his dream in the shadow of the Lincoln Memorial and four little girls were bombed in Birmingham, Alabama. Baldwin recognized that real leadership must provide a heightened awareness to the corridors of power about the frustrations and situations that the masses of people go through everyday. Indeed, emotional and physical depositories must be constructed to put out the rage that comes as a result of having skin that is kissed by the sun. It is a *human* imperative for us to make this planet livable for *all of God's* children.

Baldwin also believed (as did Dr. King) that the African-American church could provide the moral framework for this clarion call towards global redemption. Not because African-Americans were morally superior, but because our redemption had been lived *in and with* chattel slavery, freedom songs, and prophetic preaching that inspired the sacrifices of young people of all colors to peacefully demand the eradication of segregation. Young people of all hues sought creative opportunities to participate in America's young experiment called democracy. _The_

<u>Fire Next Time</u> was a militant clarion call juxtaposed with violent humility that issued a clear warning of coming attractions if certain demands for equality continued to go unmet.

Yet, what is your clarion call that sets fire to your passion? What is the springboard or platform that ***ignites*** you to make a difference? For being a spiritual progressive is a complex enterprise. One that is more involved than volunteering regularly at a soup kitchen or possessing a vile distaste for the utter incompetent leadership provided by King George II (though neither would be a bad place to start). It takes prayer and study of something other than a Bible. It takes fasting and something more than being a member in good standing at your church, mosque, temple, or synagogue. It requires solidarity and study. It demands context and courage. Young men of all hues across the world are destroying themselves and their communities because we have not offered up creative responses to stop the ensuing madness.

What are the consequences of living without spiritual fire? One is that we have allowed the dark side of globalization to capture the imagination and aspirations of our young people. A place where Al Queda and 50 Cent can offer up whimsical fantasies of violent foolishness and position themselves as relevant. No critical thinking or democratic accountability, just toy soldiers sponsored by global corporate thugs who continue to knowingly send out the sheep before the slaughter.

All of us should know instinctively that our lives are to be more than an attempt to **Get Rich or Die Trying.** We live in an interconnected and interdependent world. A world that must soon discover both common values and opportunities that permit people to reach their innate potential free from concern over the universal essentials of food, water, shelter, education, and access to adequate healthcare. Yes, this is hard work, but it ain't new work. Two thousand years ago when Jesus reminded His disciples *"the harvest is plentiful, but the laborers are few"*...he was not asking them to change the world. He was asking them to change **their** world. That is a moral imperative that transcends color, ethnicity, religion, gender, and sexual orientation. It is how we pay our rent to live on this planet called earth. The Creator wants all of us to catch on fire!!

MJB Global Chorus
November 14, 2005

Ooops! I almost forgot! Did I ever mention that I am a full-time student? In the midst of attempting to respond to all the breaking events across the world...I am enrolled in five classes and conducting research for a thesis. Oops! Those last couple of sentences were more for me than for you, but I would surmise that I am not the only one trying to stay focused while keep the *main thing the main thing.* That leads me to Mary J. Blige.

I am absolutely blown away by the total beauty of the Queen of Hip-Hop, Mary J. Blige. Vibe is honoring her with its Annual Legend Award with the fitting depiction "All Hail The Queen". They give her props for maintaining a standard of excellence and singing to the ruptured soul of a generation for over fourteen years. That's right. Mary J has been blazin' joints from "What's the 411", "No More Drama", and "Love N' Life" since my first year of college. Mary is the genuine article.

Yet, her hook was not her ability to hit right notes, but rather her commitment to stay true and honor her journey. We are fully aware of her bouts with busted relationships, drugs, and problems with her family, but her genius is in the fact that she kept singing. In her courage to sing through pain she allowed us to borrow some of her courage until we found our own. The great Italian philosopher Victor Hugo coined the phrase; "the

21

most powerful idea in the world is an idea whose time has come." I'm getting ready to sing!

Everyone involved with the complex precepts of globalization is not searching for venture capitalists to fund their next big thing. Some of us are as desperate in our attempt to create systems of justice and reconciliation as Mary is in trying to heal the world through song.

Ladu from Nigeria lost her husband to tribal violence last summer, and left her children behind as she travels in quest of a vocation not authenticated in her own church. Wilson from India is feverishly conducting a prophetic Pentecostal ecclesiology, because he knows the 25 children who remain with his wife in their privately owned orphanage need a framework for liberation that encourages more than protest. Like Mary J these individuals are undergoing enormous personal travail because they believe their songs are worthy of hearing. Their time has come!

Yet, all of my classmates are not candidates for sainthood. Rudianto left the safe and lavish confines of a 3000 member parish in Indonesia for a shared 10x10 room because he thirsts for language to offer the poor boys of Jakarta fascinated with Al-Queda. Elena from Russia simply seeks alternative approaches to offer her primary school students still coiled in the vestiges of a government that changed while the textbooks remained the same. For *Kairos* (a Greek word meaning "now is the time") is not simply for martyrs, but also for people with the fortitude to evolve publicly such that those around you may draw strength until they find their own. To sing out until they are heard!

That's what Malcolm X did. That's what Oprah does. That is what Eleanor Roosevelt did around the world while FDR could not. Or did not. We forget the nameless warriors whose commitment to excellence provided the vehicle to unleash our imaginations in the vain attempt that they would bloom into Envisions. Mary J understood this in a room full of legends Gladys Knight, Patti Labelle, Aretha Franklin, with all of whom she had recorded.

I never imagined as I was taking my Dad's work boots off that Wen Ge from China would tell me that the *post-denominational church* in China is growing faster than they can build seminaries or ordain pastors. It did not cross my mind as I was sweeping in Ed's Barbershop that I would be listening to Bob Marley while studying with my professor from Tanzania, Sara from London, and Eugen from Romania. Humbled by religious scientists who dissect theologies like physics equations, my daily prayer is to arrive in class on time while remembering on whose broad shoulders I stand. I am getting ready to sing!! What about you?

Listen to MJB as I close out. "People connect to the honesty and the imperfection in my music," she says, "because life isn't perfect. But with this gift that God has given me, I want to show what I'm dealing with, let people think,' She really wants to be free'." Go on, Mary J! Just remember you aint by yourself in need of—watch now for the shameless plug of her album—a *Breakthrough.*

The Gift of Hope Is No Laughing Matter
December 21, 2005

Richard Pryor, a man who redefined how we laughed for the last 25 years, died last Saturday. His edgy humor provided an extraordinary blend of the profane and the profound. Rent "Jo Jo Dancer, Your Life is Calling" and understand how his self-disclosed attempts to overcome drug addiction were both insightful and inspiring. I don't care what you say about the bad acting decisions he made towards the end of his life (i.e. "Brewster's Millions" and "See No Evil, Hear No Evil"), the Negro was as funny as you know what.

Even through the turmoil of six marriages, Pryor recognized his innate ability to offer up the gift of hope through laughter. Often times this gift was offered at his own expense. His art provided a medium of escape where everyday people could laugh at their reality and laugh through to thank God just for being alive. Pryor was an artist, and through his art he believed the gift of hope (even if momentarily) should be available for anyone. Might we say the same things about the current administration in the White House?

As we draw closer to the celebration of our glorious Savior's birth, there will no doubt be countless sermons and homilies on the meaning of hope. It is a historical fact that our

Savior, in his physical birth, bore a genealogy of tricksters, prostitutes, and other individuals of ill repute. It is a historical fact that he was born outside in what would now be a garage because his teenage mother and down-on-his luck father were unable to provide health insurance. And while I'm preaching, it is also a historical fact that our Savior was born into a hostile political climate led by a *designated* head of state who sought to kill Him and anyone resembling Him for fear of an overturning a morally bankrupt system.

Does any of this sound familiar to you? If I could step into my Richard Pryor voice I would simply pose this question to 1600 Pennsylvania Ave; "What the hell kind of Christmas are yawl' celebrating?" For clearly the one whom I am celebrating demonstrated in the miracle of his birth that hope was a lot more than spiked egg nog, Christmas trees, and Santa. Just ask the people in the Gulf Region.

Remember them?

We find ourselves now fourteen weeks past the most horrific natural disaster in the history of our Republic. The utter havoc wrought upon the people—especially those defined as poor—captivated the attention of our globe for more than five weeks. In Europe the suffering and devastation is still front-page news as they continue to question our moral leadership in the face of a quarter of a million people lacking daily necessities. In my seminars, classmates asked me to offer perspective to the fight that took place last week in a Houston, TX high school between native Texans and the children of New Orleans evacuees resulting in some twenty-five arrests. International news organizations once again featured police officers holding down unruly children by a knee to the back and a Billy club to the head. What is being provided for these families during this alleged season of hope?

Indeed, it is no laughing matter, as was the case with so much of the commentary shared by Richard Pryor. At a close examination of our own lives...we find out that neither is ours.

Richard Pryor won five Grammys and an Emmy award; Quincy Jones called him the "Charlie Parker of comedy" and Bob Newhart depicted him as the "most authentic comedic voice in the last 50 years." Richard Pryor was also a parent; George Carlson, Billy Crystal, David Letterman, and Robin Williams looked to him as their comedic father. His astute business skills ability to leverage his talents created a precedent for years to come as African American entertainers negotiated movie, television, and licensing deals. Dave Chappelle could not walk away from Comedy Central's $50 million without Pryor having landed a $40 dollar movie deal with Paramount twenty years ago.

What does all of this have to do with the notion of hope 14 weeks removed from Hurricane Katrina? In the Gulf Region the notion of hope is not a laughing matter. The total construction cost to rebuild the historic city of New Orleans has been roughly placed at $32.5 billion dollars. Since 2001 we have given over $90 billion dollars to the top one-percent of this nation's wage earners, and spent over $300 billion dollars on the war on terror. In the past seven days international wire services have covered three major Presidential addresses regarding his decision to invade Iraq, but none regarding his lack of imagination in the Gulf Port.

Given this overwhelming indifference to poor people regardless of color, who will tell the survivors about the hypocrisy of our democracy? If the rest of America has decided it is too expensive to offer the people of the Gulf Port region a chance at renewal, the Children of God must tell them the truth. We must tell them that our nation spent its rainy day fund on a costly stalemate in Iraq, and we must tell them that we gave it away in tax cuts for wealthy families and shareholders. We must admit that we now look like a feeble giant to the world, and that we dare celebrate this Christmas with full bellies while many souls sit empty. This is the truth we must tell those who, like our Savior, have been left outside in the inn, far removed from CNN, FOX NEWS, MSNBC, and the White House Advance team. Not very funny at all.

What is the inspired alternative? We can choose hope. Each one of us could right now muster the courage of conviction in our families and start the process of hope.

That's right. Hope is a process. Sure, you could donate money to the Red Cross, the Salvation Army or other agencies but giving hope is all together something different! Today, identify a displaced family in your local church, mosque, or synagogue. Adopt that family. Christmas gifts are a wonderful start, but do more than that. Buy an automatic camera and begin to exchange pictures. Include your new 'relatives' in your family activities. Step back from your own situation and watch the Creator unleash new blessings on both the giver and the receiver! Experience the laughter that comes with starting a circle of hope. Serve as a conduit of love because your family had the courage to make room for the Savior!

No longer must we wait for the President to do for us what we can do for ourselves. Joy To The World! For the *business of hope* is powerful and in the provision of God's peace it is reciprocal. The *business* of hope is no laughing matter. Just ask Richard Pryor.

Calling For An Internal Referendum
December 4, 2005

> *We are tied in the single garment of destiny, caught in an inescapable network of mutuality. And whatever affects one directly affects all indirectly. For some strange reason I can never be what I ought to be until you are what you ought to be. And you can never be what you ought to be until I am what I ought to be. This is the way God's universe is made; this is the way it is structured.*
>
> *Martin Luther King, Jr., Cincinnati, May 8, 1964*

This quote was offered up at the 1964 General Conference of the African Methodist Episcopal Church in Cincinnati, Ohio. It was the first time King borrowed from the famous white Protestant preacher Halford Luccock's book of sermons entitled *Marching Off The Map*. King's *Remaining Awake Through A Great Revolution* was based on Luccock's *Sleeping through a Revolution*. King would gain more notoriety for this speech, as he used it in 1965 for Oberlin University's Commencement Address, and later as an apocalyptic sermon concerning America's nuclear weapons in March 1968 in Washington, D.C. just a little over a week before he was assassinated.

This bit of context illustrates that as King matured (by age as well as by a myriad of experiences) the Spirit of the Creator blossomed in his soul in innumerable ways. A sermon initially couched as a philosophical appeal to a large body of African-

29

American church folk for American racial reconciliation later served as an international powder keg to roll back that same country's Military Industrial Complex. Do you believe that type of spiritual growth and maturation is available for each of us?

Perhaps it is if we allow God to stage an internal referendum, much like the historic public referendum staged in Kenya. For a referendum is simply a proposed public measure for a country that is out of balance with its better angels, and this week I am humbly proposing we seek our Creator and begin to engage an *entire* world in search of peace, justice, transcendence, and wholeness.

This week I am penning my vision from Bremgarten, Switzerland where I find myself struggling with the same issue of mutuality with which Dr. King wrestled with for the better part of the 1960's. As I construct global systems in my spirit, the same rote answers don't work like they used to. Having spent a weekend as a guest of a beautiful European family of the Reformed Church, I too wondered how my evolving sense of inner mutuality impacts my ministry as one who attempted to be very vocal and strident in my Pan-African theology. A theology that was more in step with history and culture than kente clothe robes or African medallions. Am I losing my edge or perhaps something in me is dying for authenticity just like my brothers and sisters in Kenya.

"What happened in Kenya last week anyway?" you might ask. For the first time in its history a national referendum was cast in an effort to amend its suspect constitution. The overwhelming majority of Kenyans voted against the measure, because it would have placed an inappropriate amount of power in the hands of its current corrupt president.

Kenya has only had three presidents since Queen Elizabeth II of England left in December 1963 to make way for the founding father of the Kenyan Nation, Jomo Kenyatta. Kenyatta garnered fame throughout the Continent for both his acting with Paul Robeson in *Sanders of the River* and for the founding of the Pan-African Federation with Ghana's first post colonial president Kwame Nkrumah in 1946.

Afrikan-centered historians leave out his harsh autocratic leadership in support of his ridding Kenya of European rule. Even as he brought economic vitality back to some African farmers, popular history omits the fact that his political party, the Kenyan African National Union, distorted the democratic process through fear for almost four decades. With a 58% voter turnout, the masses of people in Kenya are now demanding responsible governance through the ballot and not the bullet, and are preparing the way for a historic presidential election in 2006 where vision and not violence can permit the people of Kenya to make real substantive choices. These choices will allow them to engage in a system of global mutuality such that their grandchildren in 2020 just may live out Kenyatta's booming rhetoric of the 1950's. Such a maturation is a distinct possibility, because a large number of Kenyans are finding an urgent need, like Dr. King, to enlarge their territory and expand their innate rights as citizens of this planet.

As I sat in the Reformed church of Brentgarten my soul was also experiencing a referendum. Though the sermon was predominantly in German, the pastor took out a large spool of yarn and passed it out amongst the congregation. Our instructions were to go to our neighbors and introduce ourselves by tying pieces of yarn to complete strangers. Soon the entire sanctuary was bound together in a web of Christian fellowship of many colors. Very corny, until she began to repeatedly ask the question the Anointed Carpenter asked in John 5:8. "Do you want to be made whole?"

As she warned of the ills of inhumane economic structures, I was struck with the understanding that the changing of the world lies in that one question. It is here we find that not only does one's respective journey to salvation begin, but just as important is one's participation in the cosmic assignment to bring the world back in divine harmony and balance is accepted.

Now before you think I have sang *Kumba Yah* one too many times here in Switzerland hear me out. All of us have encountered individuals who have made their lives and careers by exploiting the problems of others. In this enabling we find that leaders maintain their titles by selling wolf tickets, and those who suffer are none the better. I don't know about you, but *I want to be whole.* I want wholeness for my son. I want wholeness for the people in Kenya who finally found a way to rise above catastrophic national rates of illiteracy to give real democracy a chance.

This weekend I found out I want wholeness for an unknown white woman in Brentgarten as well, a woman who stopped crying her eyes out just long enough to acknowledge a kinky-haired student in a Friday night prayer service. As I grabbed her hand her faint smile was quickened if but for a moment. Is your soul ready for a referendum? Perhaps I am getting a bit soft around the edges, but in that moment my garment of destiny expanded by one single piece of yarn.

Let Us Pray

Dear God,

How awesome is Your name in all the earth. Today we humbly come to you with our individual strands of brokenness, despair, and grief. We find ourselves inundated daily with news of poverty, war, and illness. Yet, the time has come for a referendum. Help us seek love and humor in the midst of our days enveloped in grief and wanting. Help us to abide in peace and power in the midst of constant chaos and confusion. We wish to be made whole. Comfort us in our respective quiet uncertainties, and we promise to slowly begin to unite our respective strands of yarn with others across the universe.

Somewhere Between Here and There
April 4, 2006

In a self-prescribed retreat, I have spent a lot of time listening. Listening to news reports on the calamities in France, Iraq, and Liberia. Listening to the music of Talib Kwali and Anthony Hamilton. Listening to the voice of my son who seems to possess an uncanny wisdom coiled in a spirit of refreshing innocence. Listening to the voice of my biological father express his desire for forgiveness while grasping his own mortality. Listening to the voice of God, who I can't seem to hear fully when crouched on my knees, but who yet keeps pushing me in the right direction while I am standing on my feet. All of this listening has my soul situated *somewhere between here and there.*

Dr. Martin Luther King, Jr., thirty-eight years ago today, was shot on a balcony of the Lorraine Motel in Memphis. As many of you know I am currently writing my dissertation on King's global influence, and it has been painstakingly introspective. No, I don't believe that I am the next King incarnate. Rather, every day that I read and attempt to write about him I am confronted with his courage. Yes, I am also confronted with his many contradictions, but to confront his courage forces me to honor the process of a man who knowingly and decidedly grasped for greatness.

Each one of us has been issued a ***processs*** by our Creator in which we must find the courage to walk in our destiny with unbridled optimism and unrelenting boldness. This ***process*** for King put him on a collision course with a military industrial complex that the late President Eisenhower admitted "will detour our democracy", but who lacked the courage to do anything about it. King, holding up a rapidly decaying movement with his teeth, declared the night before his assassination that we must somehow unearth a *dangerous unselfishness.*

A dangerous unselfishness is only for those who feel at peace with themselves enough to be content with not knowing. It is in this mode that your soul is uncertain of the future, but yet feels compelled to do the right thing. Here is where our souls find themselves ***somewhere between here and there*** and yet press on. It is such a dangerous unselfishness that places your soul naked on the balcony of the present moment while looking out onto posterity, believing that history in death will shower you with as much grace as God had in life.

Is God asking us to speak out against entrenched international poverty amidst excessive waste and unlimited wealth? ***Perhaps not, but God is requiring us to speak to the poverty found in the souls of your immediate family amidst excessive potential and unlimited gifts.*** Does God expect us to win a Nobel Peace Prize, write six books, and give 300 public addresses while averaging 300,000 frequent flier miles a year? ***No, but perhaps God*** *does expect us to win new friends who are different from us, to jurnal our experiences to assist others from making similar mistakes, and to speak the truth in love whenever given the opportunity.* Countless sermons over the years have reminded us of the inherent greatness that lies in service, but there is something more than that. We must find reason to have hope even as we bow repeatedly on our knees in prayer without hearing anything. In short, we must learn how to believe in believing.

As graduate school moves to another stage I am in an accelerated Master's Program with five additional students from around the world. Romania. Jamaica. Germany. India. Switzerland. None of us are children of affluence. In many ways our association with our various churches has permitted us a type of social mobility that would not have happened otherwise, to see things we would never see under usual circumstances. *God has seen fit to bless us in such unusual ways.* We are becoming uniquely equipped to offer a spirituality of resistance against the throes of an increasingly volatile global order where humanity has lost its face, all the while, having time for unprecedented reflection and introspection. What a hell of six months I have had indeed.

In conclusion, I sit here typing while looking out on the majesty of the Swiss Alps. In many ways, my soul stands on a balcony just like Dr. King. I have met the Pope in the Vatican City, and I have interviewed two of the four living General

Secretaries of the World Council of Churches. I have visited London, Rome, Zurich, Barcelona, and Paris. I have learned to love again, cried as my son boasted about his repeat performances on honor roll, and learned to accept my biological father for the man he is.

This balcony, where my soul rests, does more than merely embrace contradictions. Rather, it is a place that harbors my unrealized dreams, unmet expectations, and unfulfilled longings. Here is where I cry when I have no reason. Dance when there is no music. And laugh when there is no joke. No pretense on this balcony. No need to please here. I have the occasion to peer out over global chaos and inner turmoil with the hopes of periodic transcendence. Clearly I am leaving myself open to attack by would-be assassinators of my evolving character. Without question I am making myself susceptible to judgment by pious persons with pointy fingers, malicious malcontents who seek to disturb my peace. I am discovering that my purpose in life is to facilitate ways in which people can embrace that newly discovered space in their spirits while their souls remain bare on their respective balconies of redemption.

How am I going to do all of this? Writer. Pastor. College President. International Humanitarian. God and I have not worked out all the details yet, but for the first time in my life I am reveling in the ***sacred space somewhere between here and there.***

Or as Dr. King said 38 years ago, "Well, I don't know what will happen now. We've got some difficult days ahead. But it doesn't matter with me now. Because I've been to the mountain top. And I don't mind. Like anybody, I would like to live a long life. Longevity has its place. But I'm not concerned about that now. I just want to do God's will. And He's allowed me to go up to the mountain. And I've looked over. And I've seen the promised land. **I may not get there with you. But I want you to know tonight, that we as a people will get to the promised land**. And I'm happy tonight. I'm not worried about anything. I'm not fearing any man. Mine eyes have seen the glory of the coming of the Lord."

Let Us Pray

Dear God,

Grant us an inner courage to go beyond our contradictions. Grant us an inner wisdom to rise above our limitations. Empower us now with thy presence to unleash a stillness and warmth as we peer out on our respectivebalconies of uncertainty. We believe that you have kept us alive for a purpose. You have kept us alive for a reason. Challenge us this day to find out what that purpose and reason is. Fill us with enough forgiveness as to impart the same grace that You so freely bestow unto us. In death the memory of King's life blasts through the stereos of our spirits. Guide us now that those around us may recognize our own respective frequencies while we are yet still alive.

✍

CHAPTER 3

Ecumenical Reflections of the Mind

More Than Singing Kumbaya and Morning Chapel Services

.

This chapter serves as a tangible reminder that I am doing more than trying to find myself and engage people from around the world on poverty and politics. *I am in school.* Over the past year I have completed an intensive six months Graduate School Program with four comprehensive oral exams and two research papers. Ecumenical History. Social Ethics. Missiology. Biblical Hermeneutics. Many of my classmates were fluent in their respective languages, very competent in English, well read in the Biblical languages (Hebrew and Greek), and at least one additional European language. It was extremely difficult to keep up with both the speed and the content, but I made up in my mind to *compete.*

In this chapter two of my graduate papers have been added to provide your mind with a little push as well. This ain't vacation bible school or Sunday school; it is Peter standing on the shoulders of the teachers who taught those classes and letting the world experience their testimonies couched in my voice. My barber Ed Pierce taught me about the Vatican and the papacy. My Sunday school teacher Harold Drummer schooled me in the ways of inter-religious dialogue. Now their experiences are being provided transatlantic flavor! Ain't God good?

The subject matter of the papers include a different way to view the subject of mission from an African American perspective and the Old Testament King David in lieu of the 2006 World Council Of Churches General Assembly in Porte Allegro, Brazil. The theme, *God, in Your grace, transform the world.*

Beloved, if you are serious about fulfilling your pre-ordained destiny you must make up in your mind to compete as well. To expand your mind is to enlarge your sphere of influence while modeling behavior for individuals you may not know even as they check you out on a daily basis!

Allow your mind to be pushed as you seek to be a budding theologian, knowing that the only time learning should cease is when we are at one with Him. When was the last time you read something not as a must but, instead, as a moment of choice?

Dear God,
Is it still possible to be a thinking person and be a lover of you?
Can we question the authorship of one of Your sacred texts and still get to
heaven? Can we seek out new paradigms for mission, evangelism, worship,
discipleship, and still be considered one of Your children? Can we have true
friends who do not refer to your Son as God and still be considered worthy of
your grace?

God, in your grace, transform the world!

Allow the theme from the previous World Council of Churches General
Assembly to be emboldened in our thoughts.
For we can think of ways to talk across the Atlantic and Pacific through our
internet provider, but we have yet to think of ways to ensure everyone has
access to clean water.
We have thought of logarithms to charge multinational corporations usage of
internet portals advertising space by the click, but we still have yet to find
constructive outlets to make proper usage of the latent rage that surges from the
inner wells of unemployed adolescent men in Palestine, Paris, and Pittsburgh.

Lord, have we lost our minds or just our will?

A tempered will to find a balance between profit and purpose. A will that
fosters just as much growth in our spirits as it does in our savings!
Lord, allow our minds to be of service of to you!
Yes, we will commit our time, talent, and treasure to our respective ministries!

41

ENVISION

Take our minds and explode our imaginations to flood the highways and
byways of Your world with respectable solutions that are replicable.
Replicable such that assistance to the needy will not be
dependent on a leader or a speech.
Replicable such that the life we desire will be the life that we live.
Replicable such that the way of life we conceive, will, with each passing day
become a way of life
that we will achieve!

In your Son's name we pray,
Amen
Amen
Amen

A New Day Is Dawning

Introduction

Never were the words of grace and transformation more sensible than in the life of the Biblical character David. A man well documented for his public victories and very public defeats: to suggest that David's life was a roller coaster ride is a grave understatement. Unlike the saintly portrayals of Moses and Jabez, David's triumphal conquest of Goliath and his travailing encounter with Bathsheba have in some circles exceeded Biblical hermeneutics and become popular folklore. Scores of books, commentaries, and even movies depict an individual whom many believe to be the first authentic "human being" in the course of Biblical literature. "David, in a word, is human, fully, four-dimensionally, recognizably human. He grows, he learns, he travails, he triumphs, and he suffers immeasurable tragedy, and loss. He is the first human being in world literature.[1]

The focus of *A New Day Is Dawning* lies with a young David and his initial encounter with the prophet Samuel in 1 Samuel 16:1-13, referred to as the "Rise of David." Not only does this meeting introduce David to the Holy Writ as is first mentioned in the Hebrew Bible, but the encounter also provides a redemptive lens for those who desire grace and authenticity. As ecumenists spanning the globe prepare to participate in the World Council of Churches General Assembly themed *"God, In Your Grace, Transform The World" **A New Day Is Dawning*** provides a sober researched investigation of the narrative of 1 Samuel in light of the General Assembly's theme.

Herein lies the task; to present a practical and succinct exegesis of a Biblical giant who lived more than three thousand years ago. With David this is easier said than done.

> "The biblical literature about David cannot be taken at face value as biographical information, because it has a very complicated history of development. Also the writer(s) who put together the final product were primarily interested in David not as a historical figure but as a religious model. The historical information contained in the Bible has to be exegeted or "drawn out from its stories."[2]

For this and other reasons it is impossible to have any meaningful conversation about David without using the book 1 Samuel as a point of entry, because it continues the genealogical thread of the coming of the Messiah. More directly, it is also the first time we, the readers, are formally introduced to the individual depicted as "a man after God's own heart".

Demarcation of the Selected Text

1 Samuel stands as a book with a unique historical narrative notwithstanding its literary content. The Greek Septuagint translation first gave rise to this book coupled with 1 and 2 Kings for the volume entitled "Kingdoms".[3] (This is an important notion

with regard to grace and transformation and not because the creators of the canon have followed this example.)

The Book of Ruth is couched after Judges and right before 1 Samuel. Ruth is vital to our pre-understanding of both 1 Samuel and David's rise, for it is in the last verse of the very last chapter of Ruth we read, "Obed the father of Jesse, and the father of David" (Ruth 4:22).

It is here that we are given a glimpse of God's transforming power, as a steadfast yet potentially manipulative heroine in Ruth marries a seemingly reputable man in Boaz (Ruth 3:9b) who happens to be the direct descendant of a prostitute from Canaan. From this seemingly righteous yet far from pious union came a son, Jesse, whose last son will in turn rule over all of Israel.

As the author attempts to use the power of narrative to illicit emotional momentum and control, readers of 1 Samuel must know where the instructions of redemption are within the text. "What makes this mode of reading interesting, and not merely mechanical, is that the instructions are not always easy to spot, so that the reader is required to participate in an active way."[4]

Though 1 Samuel records the rise of David, it is far from being entirely about the Shepherd who would become King. Readers can observe the sincere yearnings of a troubled mother (1 Samuel 1:11), troubled prophet (1 Samuel 2:23), and a troubled nation (1 Samuel 8:4-5 & 19-20). Each time, we find Yahweh again and again responding to these supplications through Samuel. God met the desires of Hannah with Samuel the child. God addressed the yearnings of the troubled prophet Eli with a young Samuel who would tend to him in his old age in the face of his degenerate sons.

The crux of this saga transcends individual strivings and lies in the paradigm shift in Israel's history from a rugged barbarianism ruled by judges to a monarchial system ruled by Kings (1 Samuel 8:22). "While the *historical* dimension of these texts is problematic, the reality of social conflict over the reconfiguration of power is entirely plausible. Scholars have spent a great deal of energy in recent time on the sociological analysis of what may have been the period of the transition that David demonstrated."[5] It is vital to understand that the issue of kingship is more than merely a pious issue of ecclesiastical leadership, but a unique social concern that extends to the grassroots of a people convinced that *A New Day Is Dawning.*

The gripping part of the narrative is that the day will dawn or transformation will occur beyond our immediate vision. Even as God responds to the primal yearnings of a nation it is done (from a narrative sense) in dramatically spectacular fashion as now human yearnings are intermeshed with divine sovereignty. "Admittedly, this humanly earthly existence creates a personal story of identity, forming an integral part of a greater story of humanity which, meta/historically, registers as a story of ups and downs."[6] For God permits the reign of Saul to commence, but to use African American idiom *he ain't the one.*

The story of Saul's kingship in 1 Samuel 13:31 is a melancholy account of a once revered leader who finds himself ensnared between the passing of what many have denoted as "old Tribal Confederacy" and the dawning of a new day. Saul had all of the physical attributes needed to be successful but his few shortcomings are aggravated by his reluctance to walk in his authority (1 Samuel 10:26-27). Caught between the two worlds, one of the clearest points of contact between Saul and the passing vanguard was his possession of the divine charisma, "the spirit of God", which we are to believe formerly endowed Judges of the Hebrew Bible with the authority of leadership. "Throughout the territory of the Confederacy, Saul was acknowledged as a leader not because of his heredity or a coup d'etat, but because the Spirit of Yahweh had rushed upon him and enabled him to act as a deliverer in the Ammonite crisis…(I Samuel 11:6-7)"[7]

Yet, Saul made no recorded attempts to change his followers into a centralized nation-state. No official armies constructed or harems created. No taxes levied or courts established. Saul was simply an extroverted man who did not consider the religious implications of his actions, especially in times of emergency, until it was too late (1 Samuel 14:18-23, 15). Indeed, this did not make him a bad person per se, but rather incredibly human. So when the reader finds him keeping some of the spoils of Yahweh's sanctioned war in 1 Samuel 15:1-3, it almost validates his human position. This disobedience is castigated not only for gross incompetence, but specifically for divine insubordination of God's covenant with the chosen people of Israel. "Saul's defect was his refusal to give complete obedience to Yahweh, as obedience was understood in holy war. It was an act of disloyalty that polluted the whole Israelite community."[8]

Saul's authority rested in his inherent charisma. One can understand his later self-destructive struggle with obedience merely as an attempt to place fences around his perpetually wounded ego. In lieu of falling out of divine favor without the spiritual advocacy of the prophet Samuel he quickly finds his charisma no match for God's prophet (1 Samuel 15:13-15) or God's word (1 Samuel 15:23b).

"To Saul, the absence of Yahweh's prophet was the absence of Yahweh. He was a man cast off by God, shut up with the loneliness of his own tumultuous being."[9] Thus, for those of us seeking graceful transformation amidst complete *obscurity (David)*, Saul's free will permits God to introduce empowering *opportunities (the ensuing kingdom)* made available through *obedience (the anointing).*

Continuing to analyze the book of 1 Samuel, there are four segments in this story that, like the book of Ruth, could be read as potential acts in a historical novella. In this analysis we are attempting to permit a sense of inter-textuality to occur, a dialogue, if you would, between the actual text that has been investigated through the ages and the inner text of the reader.

"No one can read anything without this involvement of two "cultures" that must jostle with one another to strike a common ground, an intertext."

The personalities in the text include, by order of appearance, God, the prophet Samuel who we know as the son of Hannah, Jesse who was introduced to us in the last verse of the book of Ruth, an unknown number of elders from the town of Bethlehem, Eliab, Abinadab, Shamash (all sons of Jesse), four additional sons of Jesse who were nameless, and the anointed shepherd boy David who dramatically enters into the text in the final two verses without muttering a word. "And wherever this narrative is rightly practiced, it makes available that same hope that the story of David may become the story of all the others who yearn also to rise".[10]

Part I: 1-Samuel 16:1-3

The first act begins with God's question to Samuel regarding his depression and His instruction to Samuel to prepare for a journey. In telling him to do away with his sorrowful mourning over Saul's rejection, there is now the mounting of a subtle anticipation for God's impending selection. "The season of grief has passed ... because God has done a new thing..."

The new thing, inexplicably new, is this David, who simply overrides the old tension and silences the old uneasiness about kingship."[11] Samuel's divinely orchestrated journey leads him into the obscure town of Bethlehem to meet up with an even more obscure man named Jesse. God is said to have selected one of this man's sons to become king.

Samuel responds to a potential retaliatory response from the current king Saul with fear for his life. The Lord, while not responding to Samuel's fear, simply tells the prophet to prepare for a feast and to invite Jesse to the sacrifice of a heifer. It should be duly noted that the Lord reminds the prophet only to anoint the one whom God indicates, and it is here that a scandal ensues.

> "The first scene fixes (God's) authority. Tribal roots go deep. No political necessity or scheme here. It is all Yahweh's overriding purpose, all preordained. The tribe cannot appeal to reasons of the state...So the beginning makes tribal truth secret, subversive, uncompromising, rooted in the action of God alone, beyond scrutiny."[12]

God provides the prophet with an alibi or way of escape should someone question the intent of his motives. God is telling Samuel to lie in direct contradiction to what Samuel offered on *God's behalf* in the previous chapter to the soon to be dethroned King Saul (1 Samuel 15:29). The very notion of this to an informed reader creates a "holy scandal", as Samuel fears for his life amidst a potential retaliation from the current King Saul. Thus, a scandal ensues...but only to the readers.

Part II: 1 Samuel 16:4-5

Samuel responds to the Lord's request and it is assumed he heads to Bethlehem with the heifer, the anointing oil, and his horn in tow. On the outskirts of the town he is greeted in reverence by an unknown number of elders who are not sure why this great King Maker has made such a long journey. The elders inquire as to his visit as it seems as if Samuel's reputation has preceded him, and the scandal commences. "The coup d'etat is not Samuel's, nor David's, but is Yahweh's doing. It is the Lord who, taking Samuel's objection seriously, suggests a subterfuge."[13]

The prophet immediately cools the anxieties of the town's elders and calls for them to consecrate themselves in keeping with the tale of the sacrifice given to him by God. Saul simply recites these eleven words; "Yes in peace; I have come to sacrifice to the Lord" (1st Samuel 16:5a). From there we find both the elders consecrating themselves and Jesse (along with seven of his eight sons) consecrated by Samuel. The narrative now continues with the reader left unsure as to what lengths God is willing to go to bring forth his chosen king nor what is to transpire at the impending sacrifice.

Part III: 1-Samuel 16:6-10

The story continues with the sons of Jesse being brought before Samuel and the elders of Bethlehem. No one knows what is taking place during this time excepting Samuel and God. "Only Samuel knows the reason for the parade of sons. Jesse and the elders do not know that they are the witnesses of a decisive event in Israel's life."[14]

As readers, we are startled by the revelation that God has selected someone whom Samuel has not seen. Here Yahweh has asserted independence into the text and the writer elicits a kinship between the ensuing selection that is free, for the first time, of any religious pandering. Unlike the intimacy Samuel exuded for Saul, this is God's man.

Samuel continues to try and guess Yahweh's choice from among Jesse's sons by paying close attention to physical attributes. The question of whether outside appearance has anything to do with fitness for leadership has arisen previously in Biblically recorded history amongst the judges and especially in the choice of Saul. Yet Here Yahweh claims a knowledge that makes all human impressions irrelevant, and even mocks Samuel in his thinking (1 Samuel 16:7).

As the conversation ensues between Samuel and God in reference to leadership qualities, we as conscious readers are mindful of the quiet rejection of the seven initial sons; all of us have experienced some sort of rejection. "We have had some important rejections here. We have had the legitimate king rejected. We have had the oldest son rejected, one of the beautiful people...This narrative works critically and knowingly against the common practice. When there is the next choosing, it will be one of the uncredentialed nobodies."[15]

Part IV: I Samuel 16:11-13

One can only imagine the amount of time that has passed when Samuel asks; "Are these all of the sons you have?" in verse 11. Jesse denotes there is one left tending sheep, and suddenly the most unusual coronation ceremony in the Holy Writ transpires. We the readers are confronted with a triad of events that beset our mind and spirit. Our mind is drawn closer into the text as we anticipate the appearance of the one remaining son; we know the number eight carries the symbolism of new beginnings. David is the eighth son presented to us. God is about to move!

However, now our spirits serve in reverence as the prophet Samuel announces that the private assembly *will stand until the eighth son arrives.* The wait ensues. No specific time frame is given to the Shepherd's arrival, as we are not provided with a chronological reference in the passage. The assembly stands at attention for a nobody. A nobody forgotten by his whole family. A nobody who would later embellish the hopes and aspirations of an entire nation. Perhaps in David's historical memory of this dramatic turn of events when in remembering this walk he offers (as later Jesus would as well), "The stone the builders rejected has become the capstone; " (Psalm 118:22).

Dramatically, David enters into the scene without speaking. We are to imagine that the assembly has increased incrementally as David was "brought in" perhaps by his father's hired help. Immediate attention is given to his striking physical characteristics. Again, we are struck as it appears that God is moved by David's physical beauty in direct contrast to the remarks made in 1 Samuel 16:7. Is this deistic conceit or genuine admiration? The text is unclear though there are some scholars who believe both traits could easily be at work. "And why not?

Reading in the Hexateuch, we discover a Yahweh who is very anthropomorphic, acting exactly as human beings do. thus proving that they really are created in his image!"[16] In full view of his father, his brothers, the town elders, and those that brought him in…David is anointed with a horn full of oil. Indeed, the eighth son's destiny is marked for the dawning of a new day in *eight simple words* given privately to Samuel's conscious. Let us take a closer look at verse 12b.

Rise…" Here we notice that Yahweh's earthly representative has entered into a makeshift courtyard in Bethlehem not unlike the one in the Son of Man's infant coronation. Samuel (and we will presume those in attendance follow suit) stands again in reference to God's solemn internal announcement, *"…and anoint him;"* We watch the dramatic transfer of power take place keeping in mind the equally dramatic rejection of Saul in the preceding chapter. It is noted that God's power immediately takes residence within David's spirit, and verse 14 gives immediate attention to the fact that this same spirit has *officially* departed Saul. "What really happened was the divine charisma, the spirit that had endowed the old Israelite leaders with authority and strength, had departed Saul. This is the judgment of the narrator in 1 Samuel 16:14 and this sorry fact must have tortured Saul's mind more than anything else."[17] Finally, the prophet Samuel's inner man is gently reminded; *"he is the one."*

And that is it. An unprecedented transfer of power has occurred in the obsolete town of Bethlehem. Without a word Samuel heads back to Ramah. Samuel did not speak to David in this sequence, and David has not yet spoken in the entirety of the text. It should be noted that we as the reader would not officially hear David's voice for the first time until half way into the following chapte. (1 Samuel 17:26). It is here where David *obediently* submits to his father's orders as Yahweh prepares a historic stage for him in his initial spectacular public debut with Goliath, further demonstrating the *empowering opportunity* that lies in wake for *obedient individuals* who come from *obscure* origins.

Part V: Wider Contextual Interpretation In Lieu of WCC Theme

David, in the midst of an informal assembly, was granted the seal of Yahweh's public approval with the anointing of oil from the horn of an unidentified animal. No one ever told David about the Prophet Samuel's internal conversation with God in reference to this unstated ceremony. Yet, David took on the air, attitude, and subsequent aspirations of royalty. Was it necessary for Yahweh to orchestrate a "holy scandal" to pave the way for David's introduction? How would he come to recognize the importance of Samuel's action? Who told him of his inherent greatness? What leadership qualities were present in him which were not evidenced in Saul? David Gunn, author of the poignant, <u>*The Story of King David,*</u> provides a powerful answer to question like these and many more.

"Obviously the story of King David offers no ready-made answers to such questions. Rather it simply affirms the presence of Yahweh and his involvement in human affairs, spells out the awesome extent of his retribution and above all else the awesome extent of his retribution and above all points to the radical generosity with which he can break the expected order of things. In this last respect we come close to David himself. Perhaps, for the author of this text, Yahweh is rather like David."[18]

Again, the stated theme for the World Council of Churches' coming General Assembly in Porto Alegre, Brazil is *"God, In Your Grace, Transform the World."* The world is teaming with well-intentioned children of God yearning to be a conduit for well-meaning and systematic transformative work for Yahweh. Precisely why the notion of "David's Rise" is difficult to ascertain or articulate as simple exegesis. There was something inherently different about David and he knew it. David's explosion into our imaginative plane provokes emotions from both head and heart.

David's response to the anointing in Bethlehem was solemn obedience. In thinking about the WCC's stated theme it is quite apparent that perhaps this is their offering to the multiplicity of denominations as they continue in their quest for a common witness. To start your theme with *"God,"* is to not only place the Sustainer at the beginning of your meeting's agenda, but cements the commitment to revere the unmatched power associated with it. David's willingness to submit to his surroundings speaks to his character and lack of pretense.

To reflect on Yahweh's existence is to consciously position the participants of the General Assembly with a clear notion that all human activities are subjected to the activity of the One. Amidst all of the politicking and networking, simple obedience to the triune God should be our chief aim. "But wait a moment. Secular successes are pleasant... Our motivation is not to be deflected from them by superficial decisions; it would be a disgrace to return to the secular again."[19] It is maybe too much of a read to believe that David understood this, but his reticent participation should be duly noted.

"In Your Grace," the second phrase of the assembly theme, is quite fitting as the World Council celebrates its most diverse general assembly in history. People from all walks of life are coming from all over the world in the hopes of pushing ecumenism closer to its unrealized goal of visible unity. For a number of the participants this may be the first time out of their respective homelands. It is by the unmerited favor or grace of God that they have been brought in to offer their voice. "Nazareth! Can anything good from there?" Nathaniel asked in John 1:46. What about Bethlehem or Botswana? What about Jerusalem or Johannesburg? David was "brought in" from the edge of an already marginalized city in Bethlehem.

Never one to trivialize his humble origins, David's ascension serves as a redemptive narrative of tangible hope for fragmented individuals in overwhelming circumstances across the world. Grace is not an esoteric notion for inter-religious reflection and theological debate. It is a concrete reality with tangible benefits.

"Life is One. Therefore, a way of life that is worth living must be a way worthy of life itself. Nothing less than that can abide. Always, against all that fragments and shatters and against all things that separate and divide within and without, life labors to meld together into a single harmony."[20] The world consists of more than the pop culture images, icons, and fleeting ideologies offered in the United States and Western Europe. The complexities offered as a result of globalization also come with opportunities for transformation orchestrated by obscure individuals on the margin of Africa, Latin America, and Asia.

Lastly, the stated theme ends with a daring charge to *"Transform The World."* It is audacious as it presupposes that one would know where the transformation is to begin. Here is where we again affirm the uniqueness of the selected text, because the obedient and once obscure David was permitted the *opportunity to transform within his local context.* From that opportunity he would later make great usage of his primary vocation as shepherd of sheep to become Shepherd of all Israel. In faithful diligence to his work, David never lacked resources or personnel when it came to providing leadership for God's chosen people. Indeed, David's only impediment to transformation was

David. Richard N. Haas, president of the Council of Foreign Relations, takes it a step further in his provocative work entitled *The Opportunity (America's Moment to Alter History's Course)*:

> "The result is that *opportunity* coexists with necessity and urgency. It is not inevitable that things turn out right. This could easily become an era akin to the last one, defined by cold war, or even worse by chaos. But just as easily, this could still turn out to be an era of great promise, one defined by lasting peace, improving standards of living, and greater freedom...Future generations will have the grounds to be critical and then some if it turns out that we have failed to seize the *opportunity* at hand."[21]

Is it possible that a text from the Holy Writ can conjure up such power from obscure people relative to the notion of transforming this present age? Can it take the stated notion of Christian unity offered up by what some believe is a fledgling religious organization and return persons to their worlds as a redemptive organism wholly dedicated to making this harsh world livable? "They will do so if they feel that they have been touched by the presence of God, incarnated sometimes in words, sometimes in stories, sometimes in memories triggered by a written text."[22] It is indeed at the intersection of inspired stories like that of David's ascension and the parables of our Savior where our feeble localized efforts can have transnational implications.

"It is from a numberless diverse acts of courage and belief that human history is shaped Each time a man stands up for an ideal, or acts to improve the lots of others, or strikes out against injustice, he sends forth a tiny ripple of hope, and crossing each other from a million different centers of energy and daring, those ripples build a current which can sweep down the mightiest walls of oppression and resistance..."[23]

David in the Holy Writ and Robert F. Kennedy in 1966 inherently understood the premise behind the notion that *A New Day Is Dawning* with every single defiant act of obedience. It is this obscure writer's 'solemn prayer that the same opportunity will befall a cross-section of some 3,000 children of God next month in Porto Alegre, Brazil.

A Way Of Life
A Missiological Primer for African Americans

Introduction

The notion of God's mission or the study of Missiology in the African American context often denotes a sense of *someone else.* By the words *someone else* I mean that the notion of God's mission or the study of Missiology is typically seen as an event orchestrated by religious professionals or someone else outside of the laity. There are no national publications in the African American community on Missiology, hence, the reason for the wide spread confusion between mission and evangelism.

Prior to this seminar I too believed that the primary task of mission involved the development of crusades, the deployment of supplies to needy foreign countries, and the distribution of financial resources to struggling parishes by larger ones.

In this essay I offer a primer for African American Missiology in the context of developmental spirituality. Again, it is a *primer*; I will center this developmental approach in the three spheres where we as African Americans spend the vast majority of our time outside of our dwelling places; community, church, and school. *A Way of Life* guides the interconnecting of the three themes towards a Missiological spirituality of theological education, ministry, and liberation, for it is in this interconnection that a distinctive African American definition of Missiology can *start, exist, and grow.* It is my hope that the building of this foundation may offer direction for the work laity and energize both the mission and ministry of local African American congregations. Before we delve right into our stated themes, let us get a working definition of spirituality in the African American context.

Spirituality (A working definition from an African American Context)

Spirituality is an important aspect for many groups today. When using the word in this perspective, I am suggesting a unique and liberating dynamic. Spirituality involves individuals and communities in a vibrant and cyclical process: a liberating encounter, a liberating reflection, and liberating action. Spirituality is more than a personal experience in the African American community. It is a quest and adventure to discover wholeness only to be realized again in community. It is more than a popular notion of being merely emotive or cathartic. This experience encourages engagement in new behaviors, refuting whatever limits their innate God potential. And most importantly, this spirituality demands a creative integration, contemplation, and engagement for the construction of new realities.

For these reasons and more the noted spheres of church, school, and community would clearly be enhanced by a better notion of mission. We must draw from the well of Dr. Martin Luther King, Jr. as his professional life not only embodies the word mission (or the work of God), but the segment of this commencement address at Lincoln University (a historically African American University) in 1961 provides an opportunity to witness the *starting, being, and growing* as our spheres take on global implications.

> All this is simply to say that all life is interrelated. We are caught in an inescapable network of mutuality; tied in a single garment of destiny. Whatever effects one directly, affects all indirectly...This is the way the world is made. I did not make it this way, but this is the interrelated structure of God's reality for all of humanity.[1]

Why is mission so important that King reminded an overwhelmingly African American audience about the reciprocity of life through service? It is a religious rhetorical device done to create a sense of commonality, but also invoked to remind the audience of their special role in bringing God's mission to fruition. King would later continue, in the same speech, that the United States professes a balance between the whole and the individual yet practices the exact opposite. He affirmed that American society has a "schizophrenic personality", and that our global gains in technology or science do not equate with the divisiveness of our moral ineptitude.

In giving this charge to those present at Lincoln University King simply reinforces the familiar reciprocal notion of communal spirituality on a global scale. Community is essential to African Americans both in a real and symbolic sense. The inherent power drawn from community is a sphere from which all of life and life's work are derived. Indeed, King provides us with a great place to *start our look into African American mission.*

The Three Dimensions of African American Spirituality in the Context of Mission

Mission and the African American community

Among the American societal majority, the starting point of awareness is the isolated individual or family. Generally this is not the case in the African American community. The feeling of a greater whole is expressed in and through the entire community. This quality or sense of community origin comes from African culture and is carried over beyond indigenous African society.

John Mbiti underscores that throughout traditional African cultures there is a deep sense of community. The individual is born into a tribe and family, but sees himself or herself as more than an individual self or creature. He or she is born into a part of a larger whole. The person becomes who he or she is in community and not distinct from it. "In traditional life, the individual does not and cannot exist alone except corporately,"[2] Mbiti explains. Individuals owe their existence to others, including members of past generations as well as contemporaries. They are simply not disconnected.

The community must therefore make, create or produce the individual: for the individual depends on that corporate group. Physical birth is not enough: the child must go through rites of incorporation so that it becomes fully integrated into the entire society. The rites continue throughout the physical life of the person, during which the individual life passes from one stage of corporate existence to another. The final stage is reached when he (or she) dies and even then he (or she) is ritually incorporated into the wider family of both the dead and the living.[3]

Mbiti affirms that this understanding of humanity is profoundly religious in traditional African culture. God made the first human being and now human produce others who become corporate or social beings. This according to Mbiti is a "deeply religious transaction." He explains that only in terms of others do individuals become conscious of their own being, their own duties, privileges, and responsibilities toward themselves and others. When individuals suffer, they do so "not alone but with the corporate group"; when individuals rejoice, they do so "not alone but with...relatives of the dead or living."[4] It is King's mutuality all over again. "The individual can only say, "I am, because we are, and since we are, therefore I am."

It is a view that is consistent with an underlying principle of Christian experience, wherein members of the body of Christ belong to one another as well. The apostle Paul proposes that this is the very nature of the Christian community, "for we are members of one another" (Ephesians 4:25b). The Letter to the Church at Corinth makes the same point. "If one member suffers, all suffer together with it" (1 Corinthians 12:26). The African American community finds a way to maintain this basic African and early Christian belief system. The basic community and those community ties, which exist among its individual members, are of primary importance. People are connected to one another within the framework of the larger community. Individual contractual relations are important but experienced within a deeper sense of community. All communities are organized entities and contain social systems. All communities have a key institution that reinforces these norms, sentiments, and expectations. No single community is completely uniform, and all contain diversity within. But communities have members that hold consistent and commonly share goals and values. Such is the case in the African American community.

Andrew Billingsley affirms the significant presence of the African American community in both weak and strong ways.

> Even as it is undergoing constant change, major generative elements endure. The community is capable of providing resources and assistance. Any community composed of 30 million people, most of whom live in families, most of whom are no longer poor, most of whom live in families with

combined annual income exceeding $300 billion, more than 400,000 black owned business firms, some 75,000 black owned churches, a hundred black colleges and numerous other organizations, with a common history, common identity, and successful struggles against the adversities of life, cannot be reasonably defined as impotent.[5]

Finally, Billingsley argues that African American community maintains its geographical ties, core values, and proud heritage through a set of specific institutions and organizations which serve black families and people. He groups these organizations into four overall entities: "the church, the school, the business enterprise and voluntary organization."[6]

I have chosen to focus on only two of these four community-based entities: the African American church and school. Clearly, if the African American community is the place to start, the African American church represents the place to be.

Mission and the African American church

It is important to remember that any discussion of the African American existence in American society must include a discussion of the African American church. The church is the primary institution in and the center of the community. In fact, it is often difficult to distinguish between the black church and the black community. The two are inextricably interwoven.

Noted African American religious historian C. Eric Lincoln makes this keen observation.

> To understand the power of the black church, it must first be understood that there is no distinction between the black church and the black community. The church is the spiritual face of the black subculture, and whether one is a "church member" is not the point. Because of the singular nature of the black experience and centrality of institutionalized religion in the development of that experience, the credentials of personal identity, in times not to far past, depended primarily upon church affiliation. "Thus, to belong to 'Mt. Nebo Baptist' or to go to 'Mason's Chapel Methodist' was the accepted way of establishing who one was and one was to be regarded in the community."[7]

Thus, the term "black religious community" includes both the African American church and the larger community. That community exists, in large part, through the life blood of its center. Historically that has been the African American church, but in the last thirty years there has been a significant surge in the Muslim and traditional African religious populations. Younger and more politically minded people are now said to be looking for more relevant cultural expressions of their faith. "This cultural motif is closely associated with what is deemed as *authentic* black religion in its alternating phases of withdrawal from and aggressive opposition to the white world."[8] Yet, in attempting to construct

God's mission from a Christian perspective, the African American church has a variety of strengths, some of which can be measured quantitatively.

> Based on the indices of the church membership, church attendance, and charitable giving in 1997, studies have pointed out the following: about 78 percent of the black population claimed church membership and attended once in the last six months; blacks (44 percent) tend to have slightly higher rates of weekly church attendance than white American Protestants (40 percent); and they have the highest rates of being super-churched (attending church more than on Sundays) among all Americans (37 versus 31 percent). The seven major black denominations have not suffered the kind of severe decline in membership experienced by some mainstream white denominations like the Discipleship of Christ (40 percent), the United Presbyterian church (33 percent), or the Episcopal Church (33 percent).[9]

Beyond these quantitative indices of the strength of the African American church, there are certain qualitative elements that are important. There are specific qualities of the African American religious world that are present and are sorely needed among adherents of the broader Christian community. This worldview offers some healthy alternatives in the face of the many societal problems highlighted on popular media outlets across the world. Instead of a competitive individualism, a cooperative collectivism is encountered in the African American church. However, there is a rapidly growing theology of prosperity that is gaining immense popularity in African American mega churches. That is congregations with 1500 or more stated congregants on their respective church role. "...but the member of mega churches remains high, and the message maintains its appeal with those who have achieved a level of success without the burden or guilt."[10]

Yet, even within the shallow theological depths of African American mega churches...a sense of community and connectedness is discovered in the religious community. Personal worth and self-esteem based on helping others is seen within the African American context, rather than an individual's worth being predicated on his or her own acquisition and possessive of material wealth. In the face of assumed racial superiority, the African American religious world continually (oft times, very publicly) advocates racial parity, inclusion, freedom, and redemption.

While stating all of this about the African American religious social ethos and worldview, it is clearly a flawed and far from perfect institution. Like any other religious institutions it is prone to its fair share of scandals, impropriety, and sensationalism. Yet, it is an African American religious worldview that is needed, especially as we, in the Christian church attempt to challenge some of our fundamental problems: economic injustice, racism, sexism, and eco-terrorism. The African American religious context offers Christendom important Missiological elements that can help the body of Christ reclaim our much needed self-understanding. The African American church exhibits ingredients of what it means to be the "people of God" in the world today. Cooperative collectivism, a sense of community, self-worth based on helping others, and a non-imperialist redemptive Christian faith are only four indicators of its redeeming Missiological elements.

The African American Community, like other social communities, has key institutions and organizations. The African American church is obviously a primary one. It embodies all four ingredients of the black community highlighted earlier in this paper: geographical location, strongly held values, identity based heritage, and organizational life. The black community, for African American people, is a great place to commence one's understanding of mission. The African American church is one place for the same individuals to embrace God's mission, but it is the African American school where this interrelated cosmic sense of mission soars.

Mission and the African American school

Is not an education simply an education? That is a fair enough question, but for African Americans the proper African American school can represent a bastion of inspiration and imagination. Andrew Billingsley explains, "For more than one hundred years, each generation of blacks has been more educated than the one before. This has been reflected in every area of education, including basic literacy, school attendance, highest grade level achieved, and percentage going to an graduating college and beyond."[11] Education has played a preeminent role in the life of the African American community, and the African American school has always seen its place coiled in the mission of God as a shelter from the harsh storms of injustice an inhumanity.

The desire to read and write and learn was prevalent among African Americans in antebellum America. This thirst for learning crossed the Atlantic with the African captives. Their hunger for education was noted as being "well developed in the era of the African Renaissance which spread to the West African coast, that even slavery could not quench it." [12]It is interesting to note that much of the educational enterprise in the American south resulted from northern American New England philanthropy. As C. Eric Lincoln suggests: "Deep in the pragmatics of the Yankee mentality was the firm conviction that education was the only key capable of unlocking Africans' potential for the mature religious understanding which could in time prepare them for responsible moral behavior and political responsibility."[13] African Americans have continued, very aggressively, to seize opportunities for education. They have with almost-religious fervor turned education into an advantage in the move for self-development and self-improvement.

Give us some statistics, Billingsley. Shortly after the period of Northern American slavery, one third of all African American children under the age of twenty-one were attending schools. By 1910 roughly 45 percent of African American children were enrolled in school, increasing to 65 percent by 1940. In 1975 the percentage of black children in school was approximately the same as white children, roughly 87 percent. These figures illustrate the significance and great value of education in the African American community. After hundreds of years of legalized oppression, slavery, segregation and devaluation, African American fathers and mothers with Missiological zeal taught their children to believe in and seek higher education.

Between 1830 and 1900 the value of a college education increased, in the African American experience, with the creation of the historically black colleges. Today, over 140 traditional black colleges and universities exist, educating the masses of young African American men and women. The majorities of these schools are located on the southern part of the United States and remain the school of choice for some two hundred thousand black students.

"More than any other institution, the black college has provided a solid affirmation for black identity, freeing the battered black ego from the nagging doubts which were are the inevitable corollaries of a total life experience washed in denigration and constraint."[14]

The Missiological drive for education in every conceivable form, at every level of schooling, has motivated African American men and women for years. In part, this motivation grew out of the start reality that mainstream institutions were closed to black people until approximately 40 years ago. But more importantly, African American leadership has always preferred and the ownership, control, and protection of their cultural heritage, which the traditional black schools have provided. African American colleges, universities, and theological seminaries have existed today to educate African American women and men to the reality of their existence. Nowhere else, other than the church, can African American persons grow to appreciate their African heritage, African American culture, and black identity than in these long-established educational institutions. These schools continue to provide excellent role models for African American youth and produce "creditable numbers of scholars, scientists, political leaders, and clergy whose contributions to American and the world are eloquent and the world are eloquent argument for their respectability."[15]

An appreciation for African American and African history, culture, and posterity is paramount in the black school. Support for the ongoing struggle for the liberation of oppressed peoples in the United States and beyond is critical. A critique of European

American history, culture, and experience in light of the African and African American context is also present in this educational environment. Thus, God's mission for the world (in lieu of the African America experience) is encouraged through the unique and dynamic way in which the community, church, and school function together. In as much they construct a viable worldview that ensures their participation in God's mission is continuous.

Finally, the African American school enables African American men and women to experience a liberating spirituality in the midst of hostile and oft times negating larger American society. These unique schools help young people and those seeking second and third careers opportunities the chance to grow as persons and become active participants in the broader community for the sake of their extended family. "Education is the traditional opportunity through which black families find their places in life. And having found it, they replicate their experiences again and again through their children."[16]

Conclusion

Throughout this paper I have attempted to advocate for the liberating aspects of African American Christ centered familial spirituality, its encounter (starting), reflection (being), and action (growing). It is my belief that God is the one who initiates this liberation or sense of mission from within the center of one's being in the midst of everyday African American life. God creates persons in community in such a way that individuals can experience themselves, others, and God in an open ended fashion. As incredible as it might appear, African American men and women have held to the notion of this type of spirituality implicitly for more than two centuries in America. In this liberating sense of mission they have been enable to both confront their sorrow and express their joy.

Cheryl Kirk-Duggan has suggested in a womanist read that this "God is a personal, powerful, compassionate, liberating God who encompasses masculine and feminine qualities and cares for both group and individual circumstances."[17] Slaves often sang, "Sometimes I Feel Like a Motherless Child"and our slave ancestors also affirmed the knowledge that "trouble don't last always." A sense of mission was not an event to be carried out by religious professionals, but it carried itself as *a way of life* for their existence amidst oppressive realities and circumstances.

It becomes vital for the African American community to find ways of naming this implicit spirituality for a new generation of young people who feel no historical affinity for community, church, or school. It affirms for them that they are not alone, and that their mission is part of a historical transcending whole. It is imperative that these three institutions begin to name themselves so as to reassert their historical role in the unfolding of God's mission for a people who have flourished under the cruelest conditions.

There need not be another messianic figure like King or Malcolm X to bring out their inherent importance. Noted Pastor and Professor of Union Theological Seminary James A. Forbes, Jr. observes that:

> "Conversations about social transformation really begin to be significant when *everyday people* begin discussing issues that speak specifically about visions that inspire hope; when they articulate the programmatic thrust they propose; and when they describe the source of power and sustenance available to those who commit themselves to the implementation of world changing plans and corresponding lifestyles."[18]

African American public leaders should constantly speak of the importance of communities, church (or attendance in some type of house of worship), and school as if they were secular sacraments. They represent places of unity and active participation that have provided tangible hope in the spirit of family for now centuries. They do it in various ways, and it is experienced in a plurality of forms.

But the *mission, I contend remains the same.*

As we seek God, we encounter God.

As we encounter God, we reflect on that encounter.

As we reflect on that encounter, we begin to envision. We decide to act.

As we act, we encounter God. And the process repeats itself. In fact, we offer ourselves to be used by God for God's mission, and discover that God is already there. Encounter, reflection, envision, and action; or action, envision, reflection, and encounter: In the African American community it is an interconnected and liberating familial spirituality that is cyclical and not regressive. Indeed, for African Americans it is God's mission, and in that (in those public spheres) one will find *a way of life. I certainly did.*

𝒮

CHAPTER 4

Ecumenical Reflections of the Soul

When Your Soulmate is Not Your Lover - Me and MLK

When we typically refer to someone as our soul mate more often than not typically entails a romantic desire for someone that resides somewhere between uncontrollable lust and unashamed love. A person that knows what you are going to say before you say it. A person that abides lovingly in your thought and whose touch you can anticipate before their fingers touch your body. Candles only interrupt the passion that shines through their eyes and even Luther himself cannot adequately calm the rhythmic anticipation your essence knows that lies around the corner. Real soul mates…oops I forgot we are not talking about *that* kind of soul mates. Indeed, the ones that I am referring to do not pent-up ecstasy, but their lives assist in the unraveling of your stored away excellence.

Real soul mates cause you to envision.

During the completion of the Master's portion of my tenure at the Bossey Ecumenical Institute each of the students were required to write an 80-100 page thesis in addition to taking two elective classes which culminated in oral exams. My thesis was entitled *A More Global King* (MLK and the World Council of Churches 1964-1968.) The work traced King's involvement with the international ecumenical movement beginning with his winning of the Nobel Peace Prize in 1964 through his untimely death exactly three months to the day before he was scheduled as the opening preacher of the World Council's 1968 General Assembly in Uppsala, Sweden.

Met initially with staunch criticism by various members of the faculty, in the end my thesis placed the notion of Black genius on the ecumenical discussion board. It also introduced my soul to what it really means to live a purposed life of envision. Martin Luther King, Jr. was a giant of a man, because he continued to make courageous choices for humanity while staring his personal demons in the face. Adulterous affairs and heavy drinking not withstanding, King's courage embodied the radicalization of struggles for freedom all over the world. The evolution of his heart, mind, and soul That courage whispers to my soul each morning I awake as I consciously continue my own unique witness for the glory of God through Jesus Christ. Allow the following pages to whisper to your soul as you begin to seek out and identify just whose shoulders you stand on for His glory! Who has been whispering to your soul lately?

Dear God,

If we have ever needed Dr. Martin Luther King, Jr. before we sho' do need him now!

*As Israeli military forces rage against Hezbollah in the Middle East creating what some experts see as a precursor for World War III...
if we have ever needed Martin Luther King, Jr. before
we sho' do need him now!*

*As our president curses diplomatic options for the world to hear and believes providing heads of states with back massages and nicknames are the keys to unlock global stability in complicated times...
if we have needed a King before
we sho' need one right now!*

*Yet, God, we must come to grips that the King we revere in marches and speeches on the third January is not coming back.
However, the King that died on the balcony 39 years ago in Memphis, Tennessee at the Lorraine Motel is inside all of us.
The King who was on the verge of implementing a national campaign against poverty lies inside all of us
who have ever felt undervalued or underpaid at their place of employment.*

The King who found it hypocritical to spend billions of dollars developing countries overseas while our ghettos, reservations, and farms suffer beyond the point of assistance is within all of us.

*The King
who suffered from alcoholism,
marital issues,
high blood pressure,*

81

ENVISION

and severe depression
is within all of us who want a better life
but feel trapped in the one we have.

Lord, help us to find our voice as we wrestle with our personal demons.

God, unleash new visions to us as we put an end to our self destructive
attitudes, perceptions, and life styles.

Jesus, channel the same courage you gave Dr. King to reign over our
hearts, minds, and souls right now!
For we now realize that it requires just as much courage to march for
justice as it does to kneel in prayer for joy!

In your Son's name we pray,

Amen
Amen
Amen

STANDING ON THE SHOULDERS OF GIANTS
The Power of Unleashing Your Context

I hate, I despise your feast days, and I will not smell in your solemn assemblies, though ye offer me burnt offerings and your meat offerings, I will not accept them. Neither will I regard the peace offerings of your fat beasts. Take me away from the noise of thy songs; for I will not hear the melody of thy viols, but let Justice roll down as waters, and righteousness as a mighty stream.[1]

The determination of Negro Americans to win freedom from all forms of oppression springs from the same deep longing that motivates oppressed peoples all over the world. The rumblings of discontent in Asia and Africa are expressions of a quest for freedom and human dignity by people who have long been the victims of imperialism and colonialism. So in a real sense the racial crisis in America is a part of a larger world crisis.[2]

This was the very truth for their age, for their world…It was theirs to know this nascent principle, the necessary, directly sequent step in progress, which their world was to take; to make this their aim, and to expend their energy in promoting it. World-historical men—the Heroes of an epoch—must therefore be recognized as its clear-sighted ones: their deeds, their words are the best of their time.[3]

The previous quote from the Western philosopher Hegel is a summation of his understanding of the "great man" theory of history. His book, *Lectures on the Philosophy of World History*, takes the view that history has been shaped or determined by certain exceptional individuals. Historians and philosophers seeking to understand the French Revolution and the career of Napoleon Bonaparte first articulated this theory in the early 19th century. It was given fullest expression by the Scottish social critic and historian Thomas Carlyle in his essay "On Heroes, Hero-Worship, and the Heroic in History" back in 1841. Carlyle held that "the history of the world is but the biography of great men."[4] Rather, civilization was created, and historical changes continue to be directed, by certain intelligent and imaginative individuals.

Hegel subscribed partially to the "great man" theory, but put the changes wrought by "world historical" figures such as Alexander the Great and Napoleon in the context of the complex dialectic of history where even extraordinary individuals play a secondary and often unconscious role in the shape of historical events. Leopold von Ranke, regarded as the founder of modern historiography, with its reliance on primary sources over received tradition, nonetheless "emphasized the deeds of royalty and statesmen as the driving force behind historical narratives."[5]

This approach was typical of historical writing well into the 20th century, but it has now been largely supplanted by social history. It is social history that stresses influential currents of thought alongside the lives of ordinary people.

Unlike other approaches, it tries to see itself as a synthetic form of history not limited to the statement of so-called historical fact but willing to analyze historical data in a more systematic manner. A question in social history is whether the masses follow the leaders or whether it is the other way around.[6]

We find here that everyday people possess the capacity to rise, meet, and confront extraordinary circumstances given, for as Dr. Sam Kobia (Current General Secretary for the World Council Of Churches) said, "the proper space and framework." Female social historians and cultural critics have assailed the "great man" theory of history as both sexist and misogynistic. Feminist critics' view this assertion as one depicting a world made for men by men. Many women of the academy also view this perspective as one that systematically obscures women's contribution to civilization. It is for these and countless other reasons that many now view the social evolution of humanity as a complex chain of events in which ordinary individuals with both extraordinary preparation and unforeseen courage rise to impart vision to the better nature of their respective generation's angels.

A final note about the "great man theory" is that it has also been viewed with suspicion for treating not just women but also persons of color as less than noteworthy. Men of color with international acclaim like Albert Luthuli of South Africa or Ralph Bunche of America (both Nobel Peace Prize winners) to this day are not widely seen as historical contributors to the international family of humanity. This is not the case with Martin Luther King, Jr., a man whom many believe placed an indelible imprint upon both the pantheon of international discourse and civic action. "When he (King) accepted the Nobel Peace Prize he baptized all races into his congregation and confirmed the world as a battleground for his gospel of non-violence and reconciliation. He is no longer —and probably never can be — a spokesman for just an American Negro minority" said the renowned columnist Charles Fager.[7]

Dubbed as "our ecumenical hero" by the third General Secretary of the World Council of Churches Phillip Potter, King was able to impress his genius on the consciousness of the world in a way that no person of color had ever done before him or since. Yet, what caused Dr. Martin Luther King, Jr. (the youngest Nobel Winner in history) to be received with such esteem in international circles? Why in the last four years of his life had he spoken to standing room auditoriums in Australia, England, Holland, Yugoslavia, Germany, France, Switzerland, Norway, and Denmark? What is to be said of King's global influence, even as the World Council of Churches reached its alleged peak of the ecumenical *movement* during that same time frame?

It is the latter question that this book will attempt to grapple with both chronologically and concretely. In our research we have discovered a very human being with both exceptional fortitude and frailties. King was far from a saint. Yet, *A Global King* looks specifically at his direct and indirect involvement with the WCC from 1964-1968. Here again we find ourselves at the unique intersection where the "great man theory" collides with social histories more pragmatic unfolding of extraordinary events. As previously stated, in using the word *ecumenical* here we are referring specifically to broadest religious definition of worldwide unity. From this concrete social understanding we are able to draw specific questions in relation to King's global influence.

Was it the joining of a series of international events (i.e. African independence movements, and the emergence of liberal ecumenical leadership in Western Europe) coupled with the advent of technology that precipitated King's unique contributions in the late 1960's? Or was it simply his unusual charisma, superior intellect, and moral courage? Closer historical examination of the two notions would prove both factors to be of equal importance. Again, with King it was never "either or". It was always "both and." How did *you* arrive to your current place in the unfolding of events? Do you owe your current situation to luck, chance, family, or intellect? How can you change your circumstances to make a lasting influence?

To speak one's better angels, one must have the unique ability to articulate the depths of both the commonality of and have earned the trust of a myriad of institutional relationships. Yes, relationships matter. King worked tirelessly to both develop

87

and maintain relationships with people all over the world before the arrival of text messages, faxes, and emails. His interaction with individuals was more than mere opportunities for fellowship and networking. It was to push the pendulum of history in his lifetime gradually towards freedom and justice.

King innately understood the intricacies of his personal historical involvement as African American, Christian and preacher of the gospel of Jesus Christ, theologian, writer, and social engineer. To understand the depth of his ecumenical influence is to view him as much more than simply a legendary orator, but as a complex sage seeking universal redemption through the lens of the Judeo-Christian ethic. The same holds true for each of us as we attempt to envision ourselves beyond what our respective families, co-workers, and church members see us as. Instead, we must to cultivate our experiences and see ourselves the way God sees us. God has destined us to change the world from the inside out!

"Perhaps we must conclude the mysterious effectiveness of his career was due to the radical optimism of his imagination of a new reality, inspired by the story of prophets and apostles, kept alive in the black experience of black suffering and oppression."[8] Dr. Theo Witvliet is correct in denoting that the African American Church was the essential place where King's melodic cadence found its rhythm, and his praxis of non-violence found its initial foot soldiers. The African American Church was his irrefutable home. It is vital in our collective understanding of King's ecumenical influence not to diminish the inherent power the African American Church played in his upbringing. Let us now devote the balance of this initial chapter to identifying King's evolving context from a preacher's kid of a highly influential Atlanta congregation through the receipt of a congratulatory telegram stating that he was to receive the Nobel Peace Prize in October of 1964.

Born January 16th, 1929, Martin Luther King Jr. was a fourth generation Baptist preacher. His father had come to Atlanta as a sharecropper and worked three jobs to earn an undergraduate degree at Morehouse College. "Because he had to curry the animals every morning, he smelled like a mule and school chums teased him so much that he said he got a *mule complex*"[9] 'Daddy' King would become pastor of the historic Ebenezer Baptist Church in Atlanta, Georgia not long after the sudden death of his predecessor (and father-in-law) Rev. Adam Daniel Williams in the spring of 1931. King, Jr. 'joined' Ebenezer at the age of six in the spring of 1935, "because of a childhood desire to keep up with his sister."[10]

As the pastor's oldest son he grew up in a sea of compliments for his rich baritone singing voice amidst strict fundamentalist teachings in his weekly Sunday school class. However, one cannot escape King's father's dogged determination and raw ambition (ultimately becoming an Executive Board member of the Atlanta NAACP) as essential to his development from a preacher, leader, and finally statesman.

King would have many previously noted childhood experiences that shaped his racial identity and understanding. He was banned from the house of his favorite friend (who happened to be white), and was slapped once by a bus driver on his way home after having won an oratorical contest in high school. All of this and more have been written about many times over, but one must not forget that his father's parish grew from 600 to some 3000 persons during King's childhood and early adolescence. He witnessed first hand his father not only broker major grievances for Atlanta's persons of color, but he also observed his personal courage in the face of fascist tactics from the racist Southern police. "One day when I was riding with Daddy in the family car, a white patrolman pulled him over and snapped, 'Boy, show me your license.' Daddy shot back, 'Do you see this child here?' He pointed at me. 'That's a *boy* there. I'm a *man*. I'm *Reverend* King.'"[11]

It is in the personal example of his father that King witnessed the capacity one person possesses to make a difference. As he entered Morehouse in the fall of 1944, he began to question what vocation would permit him to make the kind of difference he intended to make.

King was only fifteen years old when he arrived at Morehouse, but it was not long before his intellectual curiosity was noticed by his professors. During King's undergraduate tenure an assortment of African American male professors like Walter Chivers (Sociology), Gladstone Lewis Chandler (English), and George D. Kelsey (Religion) whose intellectualism nicely with his father's mule-like tenacity.

This was particularly true of his relationship with Kelsey, because King's admiration for his father was always hedged by the unrestrained emotionalism at his father's church. Not only did King give Kelsey credit for removing the "shackles of fundamentalism"[12], but also made note of Kelsey's contention "that pulpit fireworks were both useless and obsolete."[13]

And every Tuesday morning in chapel King's mind and spirit would soar from the moving oratory of Morehouse's esteemed president Dr. Benjamin Mays, a man whom many historians believed made an even larger imprint on King's life than his father.

Mays, a giant of a man, earned his doctorate from the University of Chicago. Mays had given the controversial African American Communist activist Paul Robeson an honorary doctorate at Morehouse's commencement exercises the spring before King's arrival. What so impressed King about Mays were his timely intellectual orations and his inexhaustible list of noted contacts outside the African American church, for Mays had developed an international reputation as being an ecumenist of the first order. Indeed, he was one of only two African Americans selected for the World Council of Churches' Central Committee from 1948-1952. Here he represented the American delegation of the WCC during that time in Lucknow, India; Toronto, Canada; Rolle, Switzerland; and Chichester, England respectively.

> "Undoubtedly, however, Mays mattered most to King during his years at Morehouse. There he performed the invaluable function of introducing the undergraduate King to the universe of liberal, white Protestantism — a large network of pulpits, congregations, journals, and publishers who offer him rhetorical, political, and financial support of a kind that no other black minister has received before or since."[14]

This type of unique mentorship placed King in a unique ecumenical environment even before he preached his initial sermon in the fall of 1947, less than one year before the architect of modern ecumenism W. A. Visser't Hooft conducted the first General Assembly for the World Council of Churches in Amsterdam, Holland, 1948.

"We have to learn a great deal more in order to be able to serve the world adequately through the Church's prophetic ministry and to concrete the proclamation of God's judgment and mercy."[15] This portion of Visser't Hooft's summation of the Amsterdam General Assembly perfectly depicts King's relentless work ethic at Crozier Theological Seminary in Chester, Pennsylvania, which started in the early fall of 1948. Having been only a mediocre student at Morehouse, King went to unusual lengths at Crozier to prove that he could carry his weight academically. He took nearly a third of his courses with noted Professor George Davis and became an ardent proponent of the popular liberal theological notion of personalism.

King never wrote a paper that *specifically* dealt with the issue of race while at Crozier though. Tracing some of his seminary mentor Davis's intellectual footsteps (particularly those of social gospel theologians like Walter Rauschenbusch) it is clear to what extent progressive white scholarship would impact his quest to alleviate Black suffering.

Yet, personalism flourished in the early 20th century at Boston University in a movement known as *Boston Personalism* and led by theologian Border Parker Bowne. Bowne, a mentor for King's doctoral advisor L. Harold DeWolf, asserted that only persons are real and emphasized the person as the fundamental category for explaining reality. Finally, it affirms the existence of the Soul, and that God is a person as experienced in the Trinity (Father, Son, and Holy Spirit). King would later depict both its meaning and impact as he approached his initial campaign in Montgomery.

> I studied philosophy and theology at Boston University under Edgar S. Brightman and L. Harold DeWolf. Both men greatly stimulated my thinking. It was mainly under these teachers that I studied personalistic

philosophy — the theory that the clue to the meaning of ultimate reality is found in personality. This personal idealism remains today my basic philosophical positions. Personalism's insistence that only personality — finite and infinite strengthened me in two convictions: it gave me a metaphysical and philosophical grounding for the idea of a personal God, and it gave me a metaphysical basis for the dignity and worth of human personality. In 1954 I ended my formal training with all of these relatively divergent intellectual forces converging into a positive social philosophy.[16]

Contexts and frameworks would not be enough for King's seemingly intellectually insatiable appetite. He also began to take additional philosophy courses at nearby University of Pennsylvania in Philadelphia in his second year of seminary. During this time he became mesmerized by the life of Mahatma Gandhi as the result of a lecture he heard from Benjamin May's closest associate, Mordecai Johnson. President of Howard University in Washington, D.C. Johnson's presentation in a decidedly intellectual Black vernacular left him awe-struck.

Immediately after Johnson's lecture in Philadelphia King purchased every book available on Gandhi. He had now gained a proven praxis through the weapon of non-violence that made tangible sense of his newly inherited social gospel learnings. He would later note that, "Gandhi was probably the first person in history to lift the love ethic of Jesus above mere interaction between individuals to a powerful and effective social force on large scale."[17] King soon graduated from Crozier as valedictorian and president of his class, gaining a reputation amongst the entire seminary community as one with the inherent ability to transcend both race and denomination.

King' final destination in his formal academic sojourn was Boston University for a PhD in systematic theology. Here he deepened his understandings of personalism under the tutelage of L. Harold De Wolf. De Wolf served as both his primary professor and dissertation advisor. Under De Wolf's guidance, King plunged into the most rigorous and stimulating curriculum of his academic career. Much has been made and written on De Wolf's intellectual influence on King. Indeed, only DeWolf and Benjamin Mays would give official remarks at King's funeral. However, there are also some lesser-known influences whose ecumenical influences would later become clear as well.

It should also be noted that the indomitable African American mystic Howard Thurman was the Dean of the Chapel during King's tenure at Boston University. Thus, just as King's mind was pouring over the works of systematic theology and comparative religions, his spirit had the distinct opportunity to inhale the man whom Life Magazine hailed as one of the 12 greatest Protestant preachers of the 20th century.

Thurman was known to often reference his extended 1939 visit with Gandhi in the weekly chapel services. King never spoke or wrote about it, but it was well known that Thurman's *Jesus and the Disinherited* would often accompany him on his many trips to prison later in life.

King married Coretta Scott in June of 1953. His dissertation thesis on the divergent theisms of Paul Tillich and Henry Nelson Wireman seemed to be another doctoral project with no practical application. In 1935 the two theologians monopolized a Vermont religious retreat with their disagreement over the nature of God." King used this legendary real life encounter as the starting point for his dissertation. What is not widely known is that Wireman was the academic mentor for Benjamin Mays during his doctoral work at the University of Chicago.

It should not be lost that Mays traveled internationally as a correspondent for the NAACP's *Crisis* journal. His later informal association with Wireman provided access to a small conclave of noted international progressive theologians including Tillich, Reinhold Niebuhr, and W.A. Visser't Hooft who met bi-annually in remote locations to discuss pressing international concerns. It is safe to assume that King, ever ambitious, wanted a seat at the table.

What would also become clear was his unique ability to seize upon historical opportunities thrown his way. This talent would serve him very well as the newly installed pastor of Dexter Avenue Baptist Church in Montgomery, Alabama during the spring of 1954. His installation took place merely three months before the 2nd General Assembly of the World Council of Churches was to be held in Evanston, Illinois. He turned down several teaching positions at universities including one at his alma mater Morehouse. He instead elected to "try his hand" at a pastorate in the same state that had publicly rejected the recent Supreme Court ruling entitled *Brown Versus The Board of Education,* ruling segregation illegal in the public school system.

He believed Alabama to be a perfect place and Dexter Avenue the perfect church to impart his liberal Protestantism unto. "Mays and DeWolf, not to mention Rauschenbusch, Niebuhr, and Tillich, had all been working ministers before settling into teaching and scholarship, and King thought he should follow their examples."[18] Dexter, the most affluent church in Montgomery, had recently departed ways with its former minister the nationally noted Dr. Vernon Johns. Johns, a close friend of Mordecai Johnson, was fired for his insistent radical views in relationship to the Montgomery Busing Company.

In Montgomery persons of color were regulated to sit in the back of the bus, and the daunting Johns had been publicly attempting to persuade his sophisticated congregation to lead a citywide boycott for some time. Having finally dispensed of Johns, the deacons of Dexter were more than willing to let the young King finish his dissertation. They now had acquired a pastor whom they could train and who would keep them free from the fanfare of hostile local publicity like the previous pastor. By the following spring of 1955 King had been awarded his doctorate from Boston University. His wife had just given birth to their first child Martin III. Both King and Dexter had now achieved their respectable goals: solid worship, good preaching, and modest congregational growth. At least for six months. Little did they suspect that an African-American woman named Rosa Parks and later a *movement* would place King's oratorical prowess, his ever-growing ecumenical relationships, and his intellect on the world stage for more than twelve years. Dexter simply didn't see either him or *it* coming. Neither did the world.

Much like the investigation of King's theological development, Rosa Parks and the Montgomery Bus Boycott has received a substantial amount of both popular and scholarly attention.

On December 1, 1955 Rosa Parks refused to yield her seat on the bus to a white citizen in accordance with the local Montgomery city ordinances. Parks was arrested and convicted for her defiance. Four days later the African American leaders organized a 1-day protest to combat these injustices and create a forced stalemate with the city's public officials where they could issue their demands.

On December 5th, 1955 the boycott held, and African American leaders of Montgomery assembled at Dexter Avenue Baptist church because of its central location. They called a mass meeting that night at the Holt Street Baptist Church and they needed both a spokesperson as well as a strategy to go forth. They decided on the Montgomery Improvement Association (MIA), and unanimously elected the now 26 year-old King as their president as he had not been in town long enough to have any noticeable detractors.

Speaking to over 5000 people King eloquently combined his studied notions of Gandhi's notion of non-violence with his steadfast conception of personalism in an all too familiar African American preacher's cadence. By providing international parameters to this very local incident, King placed the people of Montgomery in a historical battle of good and evil. The intuitive and intentional idea to inject the ecumenical weapons of persuasion and coercion in this decidedly fundamentalist Christian environment also denotes his brilliant foresight as well.

> And I want to say that we are not here this evening advocating violence. We have never done that. I want it to be known throughout Montgomery and throughout this nation that we are Christian people. The only weapons we have in our hands are the weapons of protest…This is the glory of

our democracy. If we're incarcerated behind the iron curtains of a Communist nation, we couldn't do this. If we were dropped in the dungeon of a totalitarian regime, we couldn't do this. But the great glory of this democracy is the right to protest for right...The Almighty God himself, is not the God just standing out saying through Hosea, "I love you Israel." He's also the God that stands up before the nations and says, be still and know that I am God, that if you don't obey me I will break the backbone of your power and slap you out of the orbits of your international and national relationships.[19]

For something was clearly taking place in the world outside of Montgomery, Alabama as well. Independence movements were occurring at break-neck speed primarily amongst people of color all over the world. In 1954 the world had experienced the Geneva Conference partitioning North and South Vietnam as a result of the First Indochina War, the testing of the first nuclear bomb in Russia, and the Algerian National Liberation Front mounting their initial revolt against France. In June of 1955 Indians and Africans in South Africa organized the India National Congress and the African National Congress, respectively, as a result of the country's legalized system of segregation known as apartheid.

Yet King's leadership immediately gained international notoriety for his insistence on Gandhi's non-violent methods on American soil.

King continued to provide leadership to the MIA's bus boycott that lasted over a year, which ended with the Supreme Court of the United States overturning the local injunction in 1956. Persons of color were now permitted to ride where they wished on buses in Montgomery. What is not so well known are the international implications resulting from the boycott. The MIA received financial aid from Asia, Europe, and Africa to support its cause, as a result of King's ability to articulate the boycott as an international incident. His personal recount of the Montgomery experience in his first book Stride Toward Freedom provided the world a glimpse of his moral campus and intellectual prowess in 1959. In the following two years King and his Coretta would be the invited guests of emerging independent movements in Ghana and India by both Prime Ministers Kwame Nkrumah and Jawaharlal Nehru.

Montgomery was the Zeitgeist (German term meaning 'spirit of the times') for the modern American Civil Right Movement, and as a result King would leave Montgomery in 1960 to head up an organization called the Southern Christian Leadership Conference (SCLC). The SCLC, based in his hometown of Atlanta, would put his prophetic ecumenist leadership skills on display before the entire world.

Jurgen Moltman depicts King's local-global methodology splendidly in Experiences in Theology when he notes that "Martin Luther King always set the local actions and experiences of the blacks in the southern states of America in a global context. Things began in Montgomery on a December evening with Rosa Parks, but all over the world exploited people were rising up against their oppressors. For King, this was a movement for a new-world wide community of people of all races on the basis of justice. He then also met with agreement and support from all over the world, contending that was impossible to free in America as long as the Third World were not free. For him freedom was always universal and indivisible."[20]

A one-hour live solo television interview on the BBC in 1961 (on the future of Asian and African democracy) and a New Delhi keynote speech at the International Gandhi Celebration in 1962 proved him to be an emerging international celebrity-activist. The coming year would find both King as well as the American Civil Rights Movement to have reached unprecedented cooperation, participation, and funding. King's staff, in particular, had discovered the far-reaching influence of the international press corps in general and the power of American television in particular.

By 1963 the media had become a method of communication that not only highlighted despicable American southern racial atrocities, but it also continued to keep the persuasiveness of King's personality in the forefront of the global conscience of the international ecumenical movement. Television had quietly become the ecumenical triune coupled with persuasion and non-violent coercion for the advancement of SCLC's thrust. By 1963 80 percent of the American homes had color television, and its effectiveness proved the difference in an unprecedented narrow victory for John F. Kennedy in the previous United States Presidential election. For the first time since its inception television crossed the Atlantic Ocean between Europe and America. King himself best summed up the notion of the media's growing influence on his organization the same year. "Without the presence of the press, there might have been untold massacres in the South. The world seldom believes the horror stories of history until they are documented via mass media."[21]

SCLC would next conduct their ecumenical laboratory for equality in America's most volatile racial climate, Birmingham, Alabama. Six months in preparation had them for the first time with both a cadre of volunteers and money necessary to disrupt the city's tyrannical status quo. Provocation had now become a central element in their tactics to desegregate south. Their first measure was the forced imprisonment of King himself in April of 1963.

Locked away in solitary confinement, King penned "A Letter from a Birmingham Jail" in response to eight white ministers from Birmingham who publicly voiced their displeasure about the activities of the SCLC in the local newspaper. The letter was written with borrowed pens on an old newspaper and toilet tissue. Speaking to the world from solitary confinement, King again brings international attention to a very local issue. Famously reminding the white ministers of their being bound in an "inescapable web of mutuality", he elevated his moral tone and began to depict a growing desire for freedom in the world.

> Oppressed people cannot remain oppressed forever. The urge of freedom will eventually come. This is what has happened to the American Negro. Something within has reminded him of his birthright of freedom; something without has reminded him that he can gain it. Consciously and unconsciously, he has been swept in by what the Germans call Zeitgeist, and with his black brothers of Africa, and his brown and yellow brothers of Asia, South America, and the Caribbean, he is moving with a cosmic sense of urgency, toward the promised land of racial injustice. Recognizing this vital urge that has engulfed the Negro community, one should readily understand public demonstrations. The Negro has many pent-up frustrations and latent frustrations. He has to get them out.[22]

The Birmingham campaign would also be the first time in history where both the American and international press simultaneously subjected themselves to viewing the horrors of white racism inflicted upon young people. Over 3000 children and youth of Birmingham filled the jails in front of the congregants of the world.

"Millions of news paper readers in America and millions more overseas—stared at pictures of club-wielding cops pinning Negro women to the ground. And television news brought similar macabre sights into millions of homes. Abroad, Africans and European journals universally condemned such horrific police brutality."[23]

King's influence had now been used to adequately educate his rapidly growing global congregation of its universal misery; SCLC had hoped the forthcoming March on Washington King could embolden the same constituency about his dream for both racial harmony and ecumenical solidarity.

Of all King's work and addresses nothing is given more attention than his "I Have A Dream" speech on the steps of the Lincoln Monument on August 28th, 1963 in Washington, DC. With 250,000 people in attendance (and millions more across the world) it was then the largest recorded social demonstration in the history of the world. The speech was less than twenty minutes. No pointed global references were offered and King spoke for the majority of the speech extemporaneously. The world witnessed the depth and breadth of King's ecumenism live for the first time. The gathering had put the world in a sophisticated camp meeting not much different than the one 'Daddy King' grew up attending in rural Georgia. And they reveled in it.

When at the end of his speech, in a trance, by the light of the constantly recurring frame 'let freedom ring', he conjures up the picture of a new America of peace and justice; he is not speaking as an individual but as an enslaved people borne by hope for a new future. This produces a great change; the first seem to be last and the last the first; a despised humiliated people seem to be the vehicle of a new reality. [24]

The balance of King's schedule and the conjoining international scene precipitated a dizzying end to 1963. The opening of the Second Vatican in Rome and the independence movements abroad in Kenya, Zanzibar, and Malaysia broadened everyone's notion of the word renewal. White supremacists torched the 16th Avenue Baptist Church in Birmingham, Alabama on September 16th killing four African American young females while in Sunday school. King's eulogy at the funeral drew international acclaim, as he still remained buoyant about humanity's unrelenting promise. King received an audience with President Kennedy the very next day, but Kennedy would be assassinated two months later.

The world now began to look to him for moral clarity. King's written and spoken remarks on the far-reaching impact of Kennedy's untimely demise projected his status now as the moral voice for all of America. Time magazine cemented this notion by naming him their youngest ever "Man of the Year" on January 3, 1964. He had traveled some 275,000 miles and giver of approximately 350 public speeches in 1963. The following year the SCLC would deliberately attempt to take the ecumenism embedded in the teachings of Gandhi to the world.

1964 would be the year when United States President Lyndon B. Johnson would declare a 'War On Poverty' in his first State of The Union, sign America's first extensive civil rights bill, and attempt to deal with the escalation of US troops in Vietnam. Internationally the leaders of both the Roman Catholic and Greek Orthodox Church met for a round of talks in Jerusalem for the first time since the 15th century. Malawi and Tanzania were in the process of gaining independence. Nelson Mandela and his associates were sentenced to life in prison in South Africa, and the Prime Minister of India Jawaharlal Nehru died of heartache. All of these things need to be mentioned in the context of King's ecumenical influence, because the SCLC arranged press conferences or sought to broker peaceful solutions to all of them (during his trips to Hawaii, Holland, Yugoslavia, England, Germany, and Norway) utilizing a staff of merely three full-time paid employees not including King himself.

King's annual SCLC salary of $1.00 a year was subsidized that year by the royalties of his third book *Why We Can't Wait*. The book's first print included translations in France, Germany, Italy, Poland, Denmark, Holland, Sweden, Spain, Japan, and the Oriya language in India. The Guardian newspaper in London said about the book; "American politics would gain immeasurably from the kind of idealism, self sacrifice, and sense of public service which has characterized responsible Negro leadership like King."[25] As a result of his efforts on behalf of the movement he was the Nobel Laureate for Peace in 1964. He received the news while recovering from both exhaustion and a viral fever in Atlanta's St. Joseph Infirmary on October 14th.

On October 15th, 1964 he received a telegram of congratulations from a fellow ecumenical theologian from Geneva, Switzerland. The telegram contained two sentences, but it meant everything to King because as it was one of the very first pieces of correspondence he received in relationship to this great honor. It simply said:

WARMEST CONGRATULATIONS
FROM THE WORLD COUNCIL OF CHURCHES
ON RECEPTION
WELL-DESERVED HONOUR, VISSER'T HOOFT[26]

The sender, a noted ecumenist and a part of the famed internationally progressive conclave of theologians about whom King used to ruse, had written his doctoral dissertation on some of the same historical precedents to which King had given the last nine years of his life. The theologian's name was W.A. Visser't Hooft. He was then the General Secretary of the World Council of Churches. This institution had been conceived in 1948 to articulate organizationally in many ways what King was attempting do by sheer force of will. Another door had been opened. How King walked through it in both life and death would become the stuff of ecumenical legend.

ℒ

CHAPTER 5

Envision - Seven Steps to Authenticity

Martin Luther King, Jr. Ella Baker. Fannie Lou Hammer. Medgar Evers. Your and mine great-great-grandparents. The calloused feet of domestics and field hands during the Montgomery Bus Boycott. The blood of white students during the Mississippi Freedom Rides. Countless people who with every day in which they were granted the privilege of seeing the sun break loose from the clouds committed themselves to a life of Envisioning. Countless ordinary individuals who summoned up the strength to change the course of human history because they felt so blessed to be a part of the human family. What about you? As you stand on the cusp of your greatness are you ready to try?

As we enter into the book's final chapter I invite you to the pathway of enlightened frustration. Living a life of authenticity requires one to embrace your faith while finding respect for adversity. Life is more than a series of ups and downs. Rather, it is a cosmic narrative in which you have the distinct opportunity to play a leading role. Notice I said that you are not the star, but you do have a leading role. For to envision is to believe that the redemption of the world was upheld by the resurrection of our Savior, and that the daily steps to turn *your* life around announces to the universe that God is still alive! Understand that obstacles merely serve as opportunities for the unveiling of your destiny. Envision.

Are you the child of divorce? Were you ever told that you would never amount to much? Do you currently suffer from the pangs of an addiction that goes unnoticed Sunday after Sunday? Have you ever looked in a mirror before in the privacy of your home and cried at what you had become? Take it from someone who has said yes to each of these questions….*those obstacles are simply opportunities.* Indeed, something is taking place right now in the Cosmos that seeks to etch your name on the tapestry of history. Are you ready? Let's get to work!

In the remaining portion of this book I have humbly offered eight practical instructional outlines that will allow you to ENVISION. These time-tested traits have spiritual undertones and are found amongst all of the giants of the faith regardless of religion, class, gender, culture, or race.

Ingrained in my character is the firm belief that each of these propositions will dramatically change your life. Each proposal is accompanied by a bibliographic and Biblical example as well as an affirmation that will facilitate the changing of your nature.

These propositions are not a mystical antidote to sublime peace and eternal happiness! Again, they are life-giving guidelines that will assist you along the pathway to your healing and allow you to fully engage in your passion.

HIV-AIDS. Orphans in African. Global Warming. Victims of domestic violence?

In which of the seemingly endless ills of society does your passion lie?

Let us now commence to changing the world through the window of our souls. Let us now ENVISION!

ENVISION

Dear God,

What are the ways we can make Your revelation a part of our reality?

We frequent a house of worship on a consistent basis, but we are not able to balance the joys of church with nagging family members and playa' hating co-workers.

We tithe just like your Word (and my pastor) commands, but we can not seem to save up enough to live beyond paycheck to paycheck. I even volunteer in the community, but it seems as if the helpers often times need more assistance than the people they are supposed to be helping.

Help us find ways to again live with consistent purpose, peace, and power! Remind us that there is more to life than Bling-Bling or watching the game! Remind us that the pain from our past is only but the preparation for our destiny in You!

Give us Your power to unlock negativity so that we can become obsessed with making your planet better than when it found us! Give us the obsession that Apostle Paul and Franklin D. Roosevelt lived with daily, reaching the zenith of their potential while living with life-debilitating infirmities.

Lord, please give us what we need that we be accused of living more like your only begotten Son! In that way we not only become agents of change, but also become individuals of character.
Lord, teach us to ENVISION a better tomorrow for us as well as the world! For as much as they world needs our faithful service to assist those in trouble....God we need your faithful Spirit to assist our troubled lives.
In Your Son's name we pray,

Amen, Amen, Amen

&quip: *verb, to furnish with the qualities necessary for performance*

Do you possess the background qualities, knowledge, and skill sets to be successful in the 21st century? It will take more than dancing with the dance ministry to ensure that your child or grandchild can compete in an ever-growing economy without borders. The greatest tragedy of the modern civil rights movement was its inability to equip folks to carry the baton of an emerging new reality where the forces of discrimination are concealed in the growing number of people who are not prepared to take advantage of both the jobs and opportunities that present themselves. Our children literally have the capabilities to run small businesses from their respective cell phones, but are not equipped do anything with them but text each other into all hours of the night. To equip oneself means to proactively seek out the knowledge and skills that will broaden your worldview. Sadly, these opportunities are not available in many of our houses of worship.

In the age of mega churches and larger than life conferences, the historical notion of personal development has been loss to mass consumption. Sermons and music now are often provided to excite as opposed to equip. Many of the so-called 'word of faith ministries' offer up religious formulas that are not only biblically misleading, but also out of step with the cultural and political realities that many people go through every day. This is why many of our worship services resemble music videos found on BET or VHI as opposed to an engaging offering on CNN or MSNBC.

When you learn to equip yourself the notion of professional development becomes a way of life as you joyfully seek to participate in a world where your performance will be determined not by your eternal witness but by your work ethic.

How do you do this?

Buy a computer. Learn to type. Discover the Internet for more than typing, emails, and shopping. Become passionate about a different country every month. Read non-fiction. Learn a new language. Read a newspaper other than your hometown daily.

Become a student of life and watch your relationship with the Creator soar to new heights as now the Holy Spirit will speak to your mind as well as your heart. God would love nothing better than to inform your conscience while delighting in your evolved spirit. During this process of informed preparation you will discover that you have not only made yourself of greater use for the Kingdom, but your new perspective has begun to encourage others to follow suit as well. As you place yourself in a position to be blessed, your example is providing opportunities for others to be blessed as well. Are you fully equipped to handle the blessings that you believe are in store for you? What skills are you lacking that prohibit you from living a life completely emerged in your purpose? Equip yourself today and watch your world around you to begin to change tomorrow.

Affirmation
God, Equip me to be of greater use for you today. Help me to help you

Bibliography
"Build, Brother, Build! " - Rev. Dr. Leon H. Sullivan

Biblical Model
Abraham

*N*egotiate: *verb, to reach a unified agreement with others*

How do you talk to people? Without question, the reason why the Church has only a marginal influence on world affairs is due to our inability to effectively negotiate difficult issues. We have a tendency to major in minor things.

Do we baptize in Jesus name or must we recite the entire Trinity of Father, Son, and Holy Spirit? Can we combine our soup kitchen with that of another house of worship that speaks in tongues?

We have forgotten how to talk to each other! Our failure to stretch beyond our respective doctrinal differences not only disrupts our ravaged communities that increasingly resemble desolate African shantytowns, but it also diminishes our voice when the time arises to speak truth to power. Many of us confuse the skill of negotiation with the willingness to compromise. Yet, it is much more than that. To be an effective negotiator one must become skilled in the art of diplomacy.

Jesse Jackson is not known across the world for speaking before the adoring masses of the 1984 and 1988 Democratic National Convention or for his catchy slogans like "Keep Hope Alive" Rather, he is known as a skilled negotiator who between 1984-1999 negotiated the release of non-minority American hostages from Syria, Cuba, Kuwait, Iraq, and Kosovo. As tensions mount in those same regions today the Church has not produced anyone of note whom they can effectively offer as a negotiator, one who can be respected in an increasingly Islamic society. If we are serious about the future of this planet we must learn how to talk to each other. Let us zero in now on some practical steps and mental attributes that define the look of a good negotiator.

Remember that on time is considered late. Always frame discussions around communal principles and not individual personalities. Understand that raising the volume of your voice will not always ensure that you will be heard. Come to the central realization that you are not always right. Learn how to listen at least twice as much as you talk. Believe in your heart, mind, and soul that patience is really a virtue. Be willing to from time to time to forgo your methods, but never compromise your values. Trust that the words 'please' and 'thank you' will go a long way.

Become a skilled negotiator and watch your level of influence increase tenfold both inside and outside your house of worship. The Church is in dire need of effective communicators. Men and women who can rise above church lingo and ensure that humanity has the opportunity to ensure that their children's children can reap the blessings of their ancestors still unanswered prayers.

Again, how do you speak to people? Is it always about you?

Affirmation

God, Negotiate my spirit to be at one with Yours. Speak through me that I may speak to others.

Bibliography

"The Almighty vs. Almighty: Reflections on America, God, and Foreign Affairs " - Madeline Albright

Biblical Model

Esther

Vision: *noun, the ability to see through something with mental sensitivity*

What capacity do you possess to see beyond what you see? I am not talking about tarot cards, Dionne Warwick, or the Psychic Hotline here.

Can you conjure reflections of things that are not there as if they were? Are you able to reflect upon current events within a given historical time frame and speak sense to a confused people in even more confusing times? Such is the task of a visionary: to explain the complexities of a given situation and possess the mental sensitivity to see beyond the current situation with moral clarity and inspiration. It is the ability to talk in a language where both the giraffe and the jackass can enjoy the fruit of your wisdom.

Unfortunately, the word *vision* has been associated with many negative concepts and images in the 21st century Church.

We live today in a mass market culture where the notion of success lives and dies with accumulation of stuff. Car. Clothes. Cash. People are often judged relative to their ability to either acquire or purchase things. This overall emphasis has caused young people to kill one another over shoes, and nations to rage war against one another over oil.

Given this obsession for the material, it is not at all surprising that a significant number of growing churches have tapped into our latent psychic need to have more. In 2006 entire ministries are pre-occupied with the accumulation of stuff.

However, what is often overlooked by this shallow theology is that many of us yearn to be associated with an over-arching ideal even more than a Gucci purse or acquiring a late model car with a monthly payment that exceeds one's mortgage. Sure, we would love to be rich, but we have a deeper crave to belong. And that's what true visionaries do.

They speak to adverse situations while providing intellectual growth and promoting civic participation. How do we recognize visionaries when we see them?

It is painful for them to take credit. Learning is as essential to them as breathing. Everything seems urgent. Ideas excite them more than accolades. They regularly surround themselves with people who are smarter than they. Influence is more important than money. They are not scared to be seen practicing what they preach. True visionaries do more than excite people. Visionaries empower us with meaningful inspiration of what is possible if we would only believe while putting one step in front of the other. Our world is full of leaders who assuage our hearts while speaking to our brokenness. Leaders facilitate our personal growth while providing us with moral guidance to live an ethically fulfilling life.

However, you will recognize a visionary because his or her vision will unfold into your life. Yes, true visionaries illicit the creation for future visionaries. Many of us will never stand before thousands of people and speak of the emergence of a new day; each of us however can provide a vision for those in our personal square. Our families, book clubs, and church organizations long to belong to an ideal that is bigger than themselves.

Are you a visionary? Or are you just another someone looking for the churchy way to get mo' stuff?

Affirmation

God, unleash Your Vision in my life that I may be who you desire and the world needs.
Inspire me to Inspire others.

Bibliography

"Where do we go from Here: Chaos or Community" -
Martin Luther King, Jr.

Biblical Model

Moses

*I*ntegrity: *noun, steadfast adherence to a strict moral code*

Not to get into your business or anything…but what kind of skeletons can be found lurking in your closet? What would your former spouse, lover, or even employer have to say about your character?

Integrity is a very delicate issue in the world we live in today. Delicate because there are many people who believe that the number of worship services they attend or the passages of scripture that they are able to memorize equates them with a word that is many times taken out of context. Integrity is much more than that. It is also the capacity that one has to exemplify a lifestyle to the extent that others would follow suit. It is true that the greatest sermons are lived, but no one can hear the sermon without the inclusion of practical application. In times like these people want to know not only about Jesus' ability to perform miracles, but they are longing to know how Jesus lived his life.

Many people appear to use the word "integrity" in a vague manner as an alternative to the perceived political incorrectness of using blatantly moralistic terms such as "good" or ethical. In this sense the term often refers to a refusal to engage in lying, blaming or other behavior generally seeming to evade accountability. Integrity is holding true to one's values.

Said another way, being one's word; doing what you said you would do, when and how you said you would do it. However, more than that it is a quiet confidence that is passed down from one generation to the next the same way my father tried to pass it on to me. Think about what's been passed on to you as I recall a story between the two of us.

"But Dad, your crew already finished that floor," I complained as I helped him load the truck with flooring supplies. "It's not finished unless it is done right," was his quiet reply.

I had been helping my father every summer with his flooring business. I had installed floors in countless houses all over the city. I began to feel like I had lived on every street in town. All I wanted to do today was to head off with my friends. Yet here I was riding back to a job site with my dad. As we entered the home, I looked around carefully to try and see just what exactly needed our attention. The owners had hired us last week to install hardwood floors throughout the main level and I was more than tired of piecing together little planks of wood.

As we entered what looked to be a home office, I guess he saw the puzzled look on my face. "Look here," he said as he pointed near a built-in bookshelf. "There is a warped plank that is beginning to crack. If we leave it the way it is, it will cause problems for the owner down the road."

As we finished replacing the defective plank, I finally realized why my father's business was so successful… and why I had so many floors to install.

Has your private life granted you public success lately? In other words, has your integrity prompted anyone you know to delay their own personal satisfaction and install anything for humanity? If not, you best check what's in your tool box.

Affirmation
*God, remind me today that **I**ntegrity is not a list but a way of life.*
Allow my life to be my sermon.

Bibliography
"Ella Baker (Freedom Bound)" - Joanne Grant

Biblical Model
Joseph

ubmit: *verb, to yield, surrenter, or relinquish control*

Do you have anybody in your life that can tell you about yourself? Has the Creator placed anyone in your circle of influence that is able to look beyond all of you commendable accomplishments and tell you how trifling you really are?

The reason the principle of submission has been included into the process of Envision is because many of us have gotten too big for our britches. More than a handful of us firmly believe that we have brought ourselves up by our own shoestrings. The notion of submission goes beyond the glossy experience of Sunday mornings and forces us to allow an individual (or in my case a group of individuals) to have the space in your life to inject some much needed humility when the time arises. Many of you will respond to this notion with the churchy response of "is that not what God is for?" Well, yea.....but...

As spiritual individuals we are to always stand before the God of the Universe in complete inward submission. In this way our respective faith tradition reminds us that we are now empty pitchers ready to be filled with the wisdom, peace, and understanding that can only come from above.

The problem is when you avail yourself to only that one voice, the sound of your inner conscience can soon become the voice of your ego, and before long you begin to respond to circumstances as if you already knew what God was going to say. Just ask the current White House administration.

Yet, when you learn to submit to a mentor or older relative it provides you with a system of checks and balances. One of the reasons that the current state of leadership (both religious and secular) lacks the moral depth of previous generations is that we keep re-inventing the wheel. Systematic interaction with our elders provides our hearts, minds, and souls a forum to be heard in a manner that is non-threatening. And if we are lucky we won't repeat their mistakes.

Still not convinced? We are not talking about giving your will over to that of another individual, but we are recommending that you find someone with whom you can relinquish the need to get the last word. What if you happen to make more money or you have obtained more education than the person that has been placed in your life? Just remember to surrender the need to be right long enough for someone else's wisdom to enfold into your spiritual portfolio. To repeat the oft-repeated phrase of one of my elders; "ain't nobody got there by dem'sleves. All of us done had some help somewhere along the line!"

Just where is the *there* to which they refer? Warren Buffet, the world's second richest man has provided this type of counsel for Bill Gates - the world's richest man - as he taught Gates how to play Bridge and construct the planet's largest foundation.

Howard Thurman provided this task for Martin Luther King, Jr. He reminded him that the modern civil rights movement was not simply a series of important news events. Rather, it was a living organism that required serious time for prayer, reflection, study, and writing.

Maya Angelou is said to provide the same service for Oprah Winfrey. As she provides an unfiltered ear for assistance and a cultural lens that ensures Oprah maximizes a life that come along only once in a generation.

Do you have a Maya Angelou in your life? Why not? For it is only when you find the need to give up…will you find the strength to envision by never giving in!

Affirmation
*God, place someone in my life such that my **Submission** will access your bounty. I submit so I can soar.*

Bibliography
"To a Young Musician: Letters from the Road - Wynton Marsalis

Biblical Model
Ruth

*I*nnovate: *verb, the introduction of something new*

What was the time, date, and location of your last original idea? Do you recall when last your ingenuity sparked a firestorm of emotion and action amongst your family, classmates, employees, or house of worship? That's what innovation is all about! It is the bringing forth of unrealized vibrancy with such passion that everyone takes notice. Often times it comes in the form of an idea. Innovation is the fuel in the vehicle of passion that makes pit stops at an assortment of locations dispensing hope and opportunities to anyone and everyone who dare stand in its path.

This is precisely what has taken place in the information age with the advent of the Internet. Never even in the recess of Einstein's mind could he imagine that humanity would have the capability to communicate across the world instantaneously for free.

How different would the world be today if the signing of Abraham Lincoln's Emancipation Proclamation had taken place on live telecast across the world on 24-hour news stations like CNN, MSNBC, and yes, although I hate to admit it, Fox News?

The innovation of human capacity has not only changed the way the way our governments and corporations do businesses, but as it evolves it continually changes our lives. How many of you reading this now DO NOT have a cell phone? Exactly my point. The maddening part of all of the recent innovative breakthroughs is that rarely do our innovations expand the furtherance of ideals pursuant to peace and love.

Bayard Rustin infused his knowledge of Gandhi's non-violent approach to social change with his Quaker spirituality to become the chief organizer of the historic March on Washington. Bill Clinton effectively co-opted historically conservative ideas in two presidential elections (Welfare Reform and Reduced Government Spending) to become the first Democratic to be re-elected since Franklin D. Roosevelt.

The looming problem for those in the people business is that we have to articulate and orchestrate larger than life ideals that will continue to inspire long after we have left the scene. What about you?

A famous quote reminds us that to do the same thing over and over and expect a different result is the beginning of insanity. Where do you begin? Sit still. Be not afraid to take risks. Sit still. Write. Ask questions Listen. Be still some more. Submit yourself to the wisdom of your elders. Plan. Reflect. Plan. Reflect. Execute. Evaluate. Sit still. Be not afraid...

Humanity achingly longs for more than just a series of new ideas, but also innovative ways to implant the ones that are already amongst us. Continual reference is made to the notion of being still because it is only at that point of quietness do we release our weights while seeking a refreshing newness to be shared from

Indonesia to Indianapolis. Innovation is to do a great deal more than simply get outside of the box, but to improve the ways in wich we can live in it.

French politician Victor Hugo declared centuries ago "that the most powerful thing in the world is an idea whose time has come." In other words, the innovation necessary to place the earth on its proper axis is not waiting for a barrage of new ideas, but rather a *willing vessel* in which to bring the yet to be declared ideas forth.

Are you that willing vessel? Or are you stuck in the familiarity of insanity?

Affirmation
God, Innovate your will into my life
I am willing and able to do a new thing.

Bibliography
The Unexpected Einstein: The Man behind the Icon - Denis Brian

Biblical Model
David

*O*ptimize: *verb, to get the maximum usage out of*

How many times do you work out a week? What percentage of your free time do you expend aimlessly roaming the internet, talking on the phone, or watching television? What percentage of your annual income do you save? All of these questions and much more point us in the direction of whether or not we optimize the time we have been given here on earth. Extraordinary people do not magically fall from the sky. They are ordinary people whose discipline, drive, and determination set them apart from their peers. They optimize their circumstances.

Without question all of us will continue to contend with many road blocks on our path to greatness. Missing parents. Abuse. Victims of racism, sexism, or any other number of institutional barriers. Divorce. Physical handicaps or generational mental or emotional disorders. The fact remains that you are alive today! And the question remains on this day (as it does every morning the Creator allows your feet to touch the ground) -- how will you make the most of it? The answer to that question is only one that you can provide, and your contribution to humanity will determine the answer.

Richard Foster in his landmark book *Celebration of Discipline* depicts why many people from the world's three primary religions (Christianity, Islam, and Judaism) fail to optimize their time on earth despite loyal devotion to their faith traditions. He expounds on the notion that many of us have become addicted "to the religion of the mediator". What this simply means is that as long as many of us have a rabbi, imam, or pastor in our lives we will not diligently seek out the Creator for ourselves.

We will instead live vicariously off of the reflected image offered by our spiritual representative. This is why we become so discouraged and angered when we discover our leaders have feet of clay, because we have failed to optimize our personal relationship with the Holy for ourselves. However, when one sets out to make the most of a relationship with the One, you realize how fragile you are. In humble response to the acknowledgement of your own frailty, you are immediately injected with patience as you become keenly aware of others' humanity. You learn how to lighten up, because you are constantly aware of life's central lesson. Ain't any of us getting out of this thing alive.

So what are your primary steps in the pathway to optimization? How can you get the most out of the life the Creator has given you? Let me give you five steps.

First, get organized. Identify the immediate problem areas in your life and determine in which ways your faith can impact those areas. Assign each problem a portion of text from your favorite sacred readings.

Second, after you have identified the problems, envision a plan that will lead you to an optimal solution. Go beyond the superficial. What would you really do with another $10,000 a year? How would you feel if you lost another 30 pounds?

Thirdly, set out a time line. What will your life look like in three months? Six months? Eighteen months? Three years?

Fourth, surround yourself with like minded people. You only have one life to live. No time for playa haters!

Finally, get to work! Disappointment. Tears. Rejection. Failure. All of these things and more are included in the profile of one who seeks to optimize. Michael Jordan was cut from his 10th grade basketball team.

Optimize! Get to work! At age 38 Tina Turner left an abusive relationship with her first husband, penniless with nothing but her name. Optimize! Get to work! Optimize! Get to work!

Affirmation
God, on this day help me Optimize my life one blessing at a time.
Your cup always overflows.

Bibliography
"A Strange Freedom - The Best of Howard Thurman on Religious Experience and Public Life" -
edited by Walter Earl Fluker and Catherine Tumber

Biblical Model
Rizpah

*N*avigate: *verb, to steer or direct towards safety*

Equip. Negotiate. Vision. Integrity. Submit. Innovate. Optimize.

Seven very powerful words that attempt to elevate our consciousness and give our spirituality a framework to change the world we live in. Words that when placed into practice on the backdrop of relentless purpose could provide someone with the type of life that dreams are made of.

Words of this magnitude will hang in suspended animation if they are failed to be not given any direction. They each must be placed on a principled course that will ensure one is not simply spinning their sanctified wheels.

Eight, which in Hebrew represents new beginnings, symbolizes chart direction which speaks to your greatness. Hence, we use the word **Navigate** to close our journey. For as you look within yourself to steer your life towards meaning and fulfillment…it is a winding road that only you and God can travel.

WOW! Did Matthews just take the cheap way out or what! Not in the slightest. As one consciously sits back and observes the world we live in to say it is complex is an understatement.

Who is the enemy, anyway? It is not some man with a red suit and pitch fork. The enemy that seems to thwart your navigation towards greatness is fear and ignorance. When you don't take the time to maximize your skill set and navigate your course of greater security the enemy of fear has ensnared you.

When you come home from work too exhausted to make sense of the world and merely rely on what is being told to you by the media and your elected officials…the enemy of ignorance has ensnared you.

Fear and ignorance can only be combated with faith and knowledge. Faith eliminates fear because it serves notice to those internal demons that you are not alone. Knowledge knocks out ignorance because it provides you with the keys necessary to unlock new opportunities with sufficient determination.

The Creator will place you in difficult situations to gauge whether or not you can navigate new possibilities for those who have yet to break free from fear and ignorance. This is why Daniel was placed in a lion's den and Vaclav Havel in a Czech prison, because they could be trusted to navigate their way to a new day.

Abraham was told to leave his family and Ray Charles was placed on a bus at blind eight year old because they were believed to have what it took to navigate new possibilities.

Where has God placed you in 2006? Do you possess the adequate navigational codes? Or are you simply another ignorant sailor scared at sea? If so, anchor yourself down with faith and knowledge. For even in complex times like today…the God of history can still lead you back to dry land.

Affirmation

God, Navigate my spirit through storms both seen and unseen on this day.

Peaceful shores are closer than I realize.

Bibliography

"Part of My Soul Went With Him" - *Winnie Mandela*

"An Ordinary Man: The True Story of Hotel Rwanda" - *Paul Rusesabagina and Tom Zoellner*

Biblical Model

Jesus the Christ

REFERENCES

Chapter Three: *A New Day is Dawning*

[1] Halpern, B. (2001), *David's Secret Demons: Messiah, Murderer, Traitor, King,* Grand Rapids Michigan: William B. Eerdmans Publishing Company.

[2] McKenzie, S.L. (2000), *King David (A Biography),* Oxford, England, Oxford University Press.

[3] Jobbing, D. (1998) *Berit Olam (Studies in Hebrew Narrative & Poetry)* Collegeville, Minnesota, The Liturgical Press.

[4] Eslinger, L. (1985) *Kingship of God in Crisis: A Close Reading of 1 Samuel 1-12,* Decatur, Georgia, Bible and Literature Series.

[5] Brueggemann, W. (2003). *An Introduction to the Old Testament* (The Cannon and Christian Imagination), Louisville, Kentucky, Westminster John Knox Press.

[6] Byamungu, G. (1996) *Stronger Than Death (Reading David's Rise For Third Millennium),* Vatican City, Vatican, Urbaniana University Press.

[7] Anderson, B. (1986) *Understanding The Old Testament (4ᵗʰ Edition),* Englewood, Cliffs, New Jersey, Prentice Hall.

[8] Anderson, B.W.

[9] Anderson, B.W.

[10] Brueggemann, W. (1985) *David's Truth In Israel's Imagination and Memory,* Philadelphia, Pennsylvania, Fortress Press.

[11] Brueggemann, W. (1990), *First and Second Samuel Interpretation (A Bible Commentary for Preaching and Teaching),* Louisville Kentucky, John Knox Press.

[12] Brueggemann, W. *David's Truth in Israel's Imagination and Memory.*

[13] Byamungu, G.

[14] Brueggemann, W. *First and Second Samuel Interpretation (A Bible Commentary for Teaching and Preaching).*

[15] Brueggemann, W., *David's Truth in Israel's Imagination and Memory*

[16] Byamungu, G.

[17] Anderson, B.W.

[18] Gunn, D.M. (1989) *The Story of King David (Genre and Interpretation),* London, England, JSOT Press.

[19] Augustine, Saint, (1991) *Confessions (A New Translation by Henry Chadwick),* New York, New York, Oxford University Press.

[20] Thurman, H., (1979) *With Head and Heart (The Autobiography of Howard Thurman),* New York, New York, Harcourt Brace Jovanovich, Inc.
[21] Haas, R. N. (2005), *The Opportunity (America's Moment To Alter History's Course),* New York, New York, Public Affairs Press.
[22] Byamungu, G.
[23] MacAfee, N. (2004) *The Gospel According to RFK (Why It Matters Now),* Boulder, Colorado, West View Press

Chapter Four: *A Way of Life*
[1] Dr. Martin L. King, Jr., (1961) Commencement Speech, Lincoln University, Lincoln, PA, 1961.
[2] James M. Washington, ed, (1986) *A Testament of Hope (The Essential Writings & Speeches of Martin Luther King, Jr.,* New York: Harper & Row Publishing.
[3] Mbiti, John, *African Religions and Philosophy*
[4] Mbiti, J.
[5] Billingsley, Andrew M., *Climbing Jacob's Ladder (The Enduring Legacy of African American Families)*
[6] Billingsley, A.
[7] Lincoln, C. Eric
[8] Wilmore, G.S. (1992) *Black Religion and Black Radicalism,* Maryknoll, New York, Orbis Books.
[9] Lincoln, C.E. & Mamiya. L (1990) *The Black Church in the African American Experience,* Durham, North Carolina, Duke University Press.
[10] Pinn A.B. (2002), *The Black Church in the Post Civil Rights Era,* Maryknoll, New York, Orbis Books.
[11] Billingsley, A.M., (1992) *Climbing Jacob's Ladder: The Enduring Legacy of African American Families,* New York New York, Touchstone Books.
[12] Billingsley, A.M.
[13] Lincoln, C.E. (1984), *Race, Religion, and the Continuing American Dilemma,* New York, New York.
[14] Lincoln, C.E.
[15] Lincoln, C.E.
[16] Lincoln, C.E
[17] Kirk-Duggan, C. (1993) *A Troubling in My Soul: Womanist Perspectives on Evil and Suffering,* Maryknoll, New York, Orbis Books.
[18] Forbes, J.H., (1984) *Living with Apocalypse: Spiritual Resources for Social Compassion,* San Francisco, Harper & Row.

Chapter Five: *Standing on the Shoulders of Giants*

[1] Amos 5:21-24 KJV

[2] King, Martin Luther , Jr., (1960) *Stride Toward Freedom*, San Francisco: Harper San Francisco.

[3] Bennett, Lerone, Jr. (1965) *What Manner Of Man,* Chicago, Pocket Books.

[5] Rohmann, Chris, (2004) *A World of Ideas,* New York, Ballantine Books.

[5] Rohmann, Chris

[6] Wikipedia & Internet

[7] Fager, Charles, Christian Century, 1967

[8] Witvliet, Theo (1987) *The Way of the Black Messiah*, London, SCM Press LTD.

[9] Stephen B. Oates, (1985) *Let The Trumpet Sound: A Life of Martin Luther King, Jr.,* New York, Harper Perennial.

[10] Oates, Stephen.

[11] Oates, Stephen.

[12] Oates, Stephen

[13] Oates, Stephen

[14] Miller, Keith D., *Voice of Deliverance: The Language of Martin Luther King, Jr. and Its Sources,* New York, The Free Press.

[15] W.A. Visser't Hooft, *Memoirs,* Geneva, WCC Publications.

[16] King, Martin L. *Stride Toward Freedom.*

[17] Smith, Kenneth L. & Ira G. Zepp, Jr., (1974) *Search for the Beloved Community: The Thinking of Martin Luther King, Jr.,* Valley Forge, PA, Judson, Press.

[18] Oates, Stephen.

[19] Carson, Clayborne and Kris Shepard, eds., *A Call To Conscience: Landmark Speeches of Martin Luther King, Jr,* New York, Warner Books, Inc.

[20] Multman, Jurgen, (2000) *Experiences In Theology (Ways and Forms of Christian Theology),* Minneapolis, MN, Augsburg Fortress Publishing.

[21] Oates, Stephen.

[22] Washington, James M., ed, (1986) *A Testament of Hope (The Essential Writings & Speeches of Martin Luther King, Jr.,* New York, Harper & Row Publishing.

[23] Oates, Stephen.

[24] Witvliet, Theo.

[25] Oates, Stephen.

[26] WCC Library, W.A. Visser't Hooft Private Letters